Quality of Life
Volume I
Conceptualization and Measurement

Edited by
Robert L. Schalock
Hastings College

Gary N. Siperstein
Editor, Special Publications

AAMR
American Association on Mental Retardation

Published by
American Association on Mental Retardation
444 North Capitol Street, NW, Suite 846
Washington, DC 20001-1512

The points of view herein are those of the authors and do not necessarily represent the official policy or opinion of the American Association on Mental Retardation. Publication does not imply endorsement by the Editor, the Association, or its individual members.

Printed in the United States of America.

Library of Congress Cataloging-in-Publication Data
Quality of life/edited by Robert L. Schalock.
     p.   cm.
  Includes bibliographical references.
  ISBN 0-940898-38-1
    1. Mentally handicapped—Services for—United States. 2. Mental retardation—United States. 3. Quality of Life—United States. 4. Quality of Life—Measurement. I. Schalock, Robert L. II. American Association on Mental Retardation.
HV3006.A4Q34 1995   95-50087
362.3'8'0973 — dc20   CIP

Contents

Contributors

Robert Bogdan
The Center on Human Policy
Syracuse University
School of Education
200 Huntington Hall
Syracuse, NY 13244-2340

Sharon A. Borthwick-Duffy
School of Education
University of California
Riverside, CA 92521

Robert B. Edgerton
UCLA-NPI
760 Westwood Plaza
Los Angeles, CA 90024

Earl Faulkner
Meyer Rehabilitation Institute
University of Nebraska Medical Center
42nd and Dewey Avenues
Omaha, NE 68198

David Felce
Professor of Research in Learning Disabilities
Welsh Centre for Learning Disabilities
    Applied Research Unit
Meridian Court
North Road
Cardiff CF4 3BL
Wales UK

Cathy Ficker Terrill
Vice President
Quality and Strategic Planning
Ray Graham Association for People with
    Disabilities
340 W. Butterfield
Elmhurst, IL 60126

Charles A. Gardner
Hastings College
Hastings, NE 68901

Laird W. Heal
Transition Research Institute
University of Illinois at Urbana-Champaign
113 Children's Research Center
51 Gerty Drive
Champaign, IL 61820

Carolyn Hughes
Department of Special Education
Peabody College
Vanderbilt University
Nashville, TN 37203

Bogseon Hwang
Department of Special Education
Peabody College
Vanderbilt University
Nashville, TN 37203

Kenneth D. Keith
Department of Psychology
Nebraska Wesleyan University
Lincoln, NE 68504-2796

Jonathan Perry
Welsh Centre for Learning Disabilities
    Applied Research Unit
Meridian Court
North Road
Cardiff CF4 3BL
Wales UK

Robert L. Schalock
Department of Psychology
Hastings College
Hastings, NE 68901

Carol Sigelman
Department of Psychology
George Washington University
Washington, DC 20052

Jack Stark
Physicians Clinic
10060 Regency Circle
Omaha, NE 68114

Steven J. Taylor
Professor
The Center on Human Policy
Syracuse University
School of Education
200 Huntington Hall
Syracuse, NY 13244-2340

Nancy A. Ward
People First of Nebraska
2401 N. Street
Suite 411
Lincoln, NE 68510

Preface

Quality of life is not a new concept; indeed, since antiquity people have pursued the dimensions of a life of quality. As one reviewer of this manuscript stated, "maximizing the quality of life is a human ambition, perhaps universal in nature, but its form is individually unique." The concept is also not new to the field of mental retardation, as another reviewer wrote:

> *...The elements of quality of life have been embodied and measured in adaptive behavior scales, accreditation standards, and program development goals and guidelines. Factors bearing directly on quality of life have been studied in post-institutional adjustment, community placements, rehabilitation outcomes, and many others. They are also inherent in greater or lesser degree in the concepts of normalization, mainstreaming, and integration.*

What is different today—and what makes the concept of quality of life so important to our field—is our attempt to use this concept as a process and an overriding principle to improve the lives of persons with mental retardation and closely related disabilities, and to evaluate the social validity of current (re)habilitation efforts. To do so requires a clear understanding of the concept and a valid approach to its measurement. Clarifying these two issues, in the light of significant advances in our understanding over the past several years, is the primary purpose of this volume.

Quality of life is a complex concept due to its multiple perspectives and dimensions, and to the fact that it can be operationalized in many different ways. Thus, there is a strong need for continued discussion, debates, and updates. Furthermore, this is a critical time in both the history of approaches to persons with mental retardation and closely related disabilities, and in how our society views people who are different by any criterion. As a research construct and sensitizing principle, quality of life is applicable to society as a whole and thus is a potentially valuable bridge to common understanding and good.

It is a sad fact that people with disabilities are vulnerable to shifting social, political, and economic trends. For example, the current social transformation is predicted to result in a 21st century economic order in which knowledge, not labor, raw materials, or capital, will be the key resource; a social order in which inequality based on knowledge will be the major challenge; and a public policy in which government cannot be expected to solve social and economic problems (Drucker, 1994). What general principle should underlie this transformation with regard to its impact on people with mental retardation and closely related disabilities? I suggest that the concept of quality of life provides a fundamentally positive and growth-oriented principle that can be the basis for developing a national and international policy on disability. Although it may be used for the wrong reasons (Cf. Luckasson, 1990; Wolfensberger, 1994), the concept steers us in the right direction: towards person-centered planning and support. Throughout this volume, the recurrent theme is well-being, opportunities to fulfill potential, and commitment to positive social involvement.

We in the disabilities field have been part of a paradigm shift in how we view and interact with persons with mental retardation and closely related disabilities. The following aspects of that shift underscore the importance of a clear understanding of the concept of quality of life and its measurement:

1. A transformed vision of what constitutes the life possibilities of persons with mental retardation. This view includes an emphasis on self-determination, strengths and capabilities, importance of normalized and typical environments, provision of individualized support systems, enhanced adaptive behavior and role status, and equity (Luckasson et al., 1992).

2. A supports paradigm that underlies service delivery to persons with disabilities and focuses on sup-

ported living, employment, and inclusive education (Bradley, Ashbaugh, & Blaney, 1994; Smull & Danehey, 1994).

3. An interfacing of the concept of quality of life with quality enhancement, quality assurance, quality management, and outcome-based evaluation (Albin, 1992; Buckley & Mank, 1994; Schalock, 1994, 1995).

Overall, since the emergence of the quality of life as a principle in human services, interest in the concept has grown. There have been increases in research into its critical consensual dimensions, in use of multidimensional measurement techniques, and in applications in program delivery and evaluation efforts. There has also been a tendency toward conceptualizing quality of life as a process or flow. Despite these efforts, there are still gaps in our knowledge. Public policy and (re)habilitation organizations are struggling to reformulate themselves within a quality of life paradigm that reflects the quality revolution. Policy developers and program administrators need the most current thinking about the concept of quality of life and its measurement in order to improve services and promote rational public policies. Helping to fill these knowledge gaps and provide policymakers and service providers with up-to-date information is the purpose of this book.

The volume began as a simple revision of the book on quality of life published by the American Association on Mental Retardation in 1990 (Schalock). When contributors were invited to update their chapters, many responded with new material and significantly different conceptualizations. Thus, it became apparent that a new book should be developed, and in fact, the manuscript grew into two distinct volumes: this one on the conceptualization and measurement of quality of life, and a second on the application of the concept in services for persons with disabilities. Volume I focuses on quality of life as a sensitizing concept and a research construct. Volume II focuses on service delivery, stressing the impact of the quality of life concept on the current paradigm shift in mental retardation services.

The reader will also find here three chapters that remain essentially unchanged from the 1990 publication. One reminds us of the continuing importance of viewing quality of life from the individual's perspective, and two reflect minor updates of key measurement principles and approaches to quality of life.

Throughout the development of this volume, I have had the privilege to once again work with a group of colleagues whom I respect highly and from whom I have learned much. Throughout the editing and revision process, I have also appreciated the excellent editorial assistance from Dr. Gary Siperstein, AAMR Book and Monograph Editor, and the four external reviewers who provided me with extensive and helpful suggestions. I dedicate the volume to the people who are asking for and expecting an enhanced quality of life, and to my colleagues and friends who support them in their efforts.

Robert L. Schalock, Ph.D.

References

Albin, J.M. (1992). *Quality improvement in employment and other human services: Managing for quality through change*. Baltimore: Brookes.

Bradley, V.J., Ashbaugh, J.W., & Blaney, B.C. (1994). *Creating individual supports for people with developmental disabilities: A mandate for change at many levels*. Baltimore: Brookes.

Buckley, J., & Mank, D. (1994). New perspectives on training and technical assistance: Moving from assumptions to a focus on quality. *Journal of the Association for Persons with Severe Handicaps, 19,* 223-232.

Drucker, P.F. (1994, November). The age of social transformation. *The Atlantic Monthly,* 53-80.

Luckasson, R. (1990). A lawyer's perspective on quality of life. In R.L. Schalock, (Ed.), *Quality of life: Perspectives and issues* (pp. 211-215). Washington, DC: American Association on Mental Retardation.

Luckasson, R., Coulter, D.L., Polloway, E.A., Reiss, S., Schalock, R.L., Snell, M.E., Spitalnik, D.M., & Stark, J.A. (1992). *Mental retardation: Definition, classification and systems of supports*. Washington, DC: American Association on Mental Retardation.

Schalock, R.L. (Ed.). (1990). *Quality of life: Perspectives and issues*. Washington, DC: American Association on Mental Retardation.

Schalock, R.L. (1994). Quality of life, quality enhancement, and quality of assurance: Implications for program planning and evaluation in the field of mental retardation and developmental disabilities. *Evaluation and Program Planning, 17,* (2), 121-131.

Schalock, R.L. (1995). *Outcome-based evaluation.* New York: Plenum Publishing Corporation.

Smull, M.W., & Danehey, A.J. (1994). Increasing quality while reducing cost: The challenges of the 1990s. In V.J. Bradley, J.W. Ashbaugh, & B.C. Blaney (Eds.), *Creating individual supports for people with developmental disabilities: A mandate for change at many levels* (pp. 59-78). Baltimore: Brookes.

Wolfensberger, W. (1994). Let's hang up "quality of life" as a hopeless term. In D.A. Goode (Ed.), *Quality of life for persons with disabilities: International perspectives and issues* (pp. 285-321). Cambridge, MA: Brookline Books.

Part I

The Conceptualization of Quality of Life

The concept of quality of life can be considered a sensitizing concept that gives us a general sense of reference and guidance from the individual's perspective in approaching an emerging sociopolitical movement. We begin our odyssey into the conceptualization and measurement of the quality of life concept with five chapters written by self-advocates, family members, and advocates for persons with mental retardation. These authors share their very different perspectives on the sensitizing aspects of quality of life.

Self-advocates sensitize the disability community to the importance of people with disabilities speaking for themselves, exercising their rights and responsibilities, organizing, and working together to create opportunities for personal growth and development. Family members sensitize us to the need for quality services provided in natural settings, flexibility in service and supports options, interdependence among community members, choices and empowerment, health and safety, and understanding relationships. Similarly, advocates for persons with mental retardation sensitize us to several facts: the concept of quality of life has no meaning apart from the subjective experiences of the individual; quality of life may be experienced differently by different people; the study of a person's quality of life requires in-depth knowledge of the person; a person's individual choice is *the* guiding principle to enhance the quality of life; and an understanding of quality of life cannot be separated from developmental stages, support networks, and relevant life domains.

Each author approaches these issues differently. Each has been impacted by both a condition and a culture and is in a unique position to sensitize us to the multifaceted, subjective nature of the quality of life concept and thereby help us understand better its conceptualization and meaning.

We begin with a chapter by Nancy Ward, who has been instrumental in the self-advocacy movement. In the 1990 publication, *Quality of Life,* Nancy discussed how she felt about her new life in the community. In this chapter, she discusses her role in the self-advocacy movement and talks about the importance of equity and empowerment. She shares her dream of the future, which is to "…work myself out of a job, because there will be no need for organizations that work with people who have a disability. People with a disability will be accepted like everyone else, so there won't be a need for those kinds of organizations. That is my dream."

Steve Taylor and Robert Bogdan remind us in Chapter 2 that quality of life must be studied from the perspective of the individual, including taking a personal perspective and acquiring an in-depth knowledge of the person. They also present a number of basic principles that one should keep in mind while reading this first section: (a) quality of life must be understood in terms of people's subjective experiences; (b) quality of life may be experienced differently by different people; (c) the study of the quality of life of people labelled "mentally retarded" requires that the label be set aside; (d) an inquiry into the quality of life of people with mental retardation requires looking at the world from their perspectives; and (e) definitions and conceptions of quality of life must respect people's subjective experiences.

This theme is continued in the chapter by Jack Stark and Earl Faulkner, who use a life-span perspective in their conceptualization. They also caution us that a person's perception of a life of quality is a dynamic process, influenced greatly by developmental stage, supports provided, and respective life domain such as health care, living environment, family, social and emotional relationships, educational environment and opportunities, work, and leisure.

A parent's perspective is essential to understanding the meaning of quality of life and sensitizing us to its multiple dimensions. Cathy Ficker-Terrill wonders why human services cannot be more consumer-referenced and quality-oriented. She goes on to define quality for us in reference to several aspects of services: location (natural settings), community participation, choices, safety, economic security, and health. Throughout the chapter, she stresses the need to enhance service quality and defines quality mainly in terms of consumer perceptions.

The importance of relationships to a life of quality is described beautifully in the last chapter in this section from a grandparent's perspective. Charlie Gardner stresses that one should begin with the family's view of quality of life and then progress to its measurement and implementation. Note also the key role that relationships play in quality of life, as reflected in a description of what transpires as he drives his granddaughter to her physical therapy.

> *This eight-mile journey is a precious time for me because we get a chance to be alone together without interruptions. It's a time to visit, tell jokes, and find out how school is going... Although the verbalization is strictly one-way, the communication is definitely two-way. I learned a long time ago that Laura hears and understands far more than a casual observer would guess.*

In reading these five chapters, pay close attention to the subjective quality of the concept of quality of life. What the contributors of this section are saying is that quality of life is best conceptualized as a sensitizing concept that is best understood from the perspective of the individual and requires in-depth knowledge of the individual; embodies general feelings of well-being, opportunities to fulfill one's hopes and dreams, and positive social interactions; cannot be separated from one's developmental stage, support network, and relevant life domains; and gives us a sense of reference and guidance in approaching quality of life issues.

C H A P T E R   1

Self-Advocacy: Foundation for Quality of Life

Nancy A. Ward
People First of Nebraska

Kenneth D. Keith
Nebraska Wesleyan University

Nancy Ward is national chairperson of Self-Advocates Becoming Empowered, a country-wide self-advocacy organization in the United States, and former president of People First of Nebraska. In her staff role as self-advocacy organizer for People First of Nebraska, she works to establish new chapters and to assist others to speak out on their own behalf. In this conversation with Ken Keith, Nancy discusses the self-advocacy movement, why self-advocacy is a foundation for one's quality of life, and her own views of the future of self-advocacy.

—Editor

Keith: Nancy, I know that for many years you have been active in the self-advocacy movement, not only in Nebraska, but across the United States. What is it in your experience that makes your self-advocacy skills so important to you?

Ward: At one time, I did not see myself as a person because of all the labels that people put on someone with a disability. I didn't have the confidence to speak up, especially in front of people. Being able to do that is important to me, because I think it's important for other people to understand how people with disabilities feel about being labeled. So now that I have a chance to go across the country, I can be an example for people, showing them how they can speak up for themselves, so it won't take them five years to learn, like it did for me.

> *If you think you are handicapped you might as well stay indoors.*
> *If you think you are a person, come out and tell the world.*
>
> **—Raymond Loomis**
> **(William & Shoultz, 1982, p. 17)**

Keith: You say that it took you five years to learn to speak for yourself. Tell me a little about what happened during those five years in your life that made it possible for you to be able to speak out for yourself.

Ward: I think it's very important for people with disabilities to learn to accept and understand their disability, because when they are able to do that, they will see themselves as persons. A few years ago, I saw a commercial on TV; it was about Special Olympics, and these kids were being paraded across a stage in a way that made people feel sorry for them to raise money. To me, the worst thing you can do to someone who has a disability is to pity them—you will see them as a kid for the rest of their life, and you will never let them grow up. They will never be what they can be, because you will see their disability rather than their capabilities.

So I got mad at the TV and I yelled at the TV. Well, it doesn't do a lot of good to yell at a TV! So some of my friends talked to me about becoming a member of Advocacy First of Lincoln—the local People First chapter at that time. We wrote a letter to President Carter and the Kennedy Foundation about our concerns regarding the commercial, and they took it off the air. This showed me how to direct my feelings in a positive way; before, I only knew how to direct them in a negative way.

Keith: Since that time, People First has become a significant part of your life and the lives of many other people. I want to ask you to talk a bit about People First. What is it? Who is it? What is its role?

Ward: Most of the states across the country have some type of organized self-advocacy. People First of Nebraska is the self-advocacy organization in my state. It teaches people with disabilities how to speak out for themselves. It

teaches us our rights, but along with that, it teaches us our responsibilities. I think it's important that people with disabilities learn responsibilities as well as rights, because if we want to be treated the same as everybody else, we need to know and experience the consequences of our actions.

For example, when I talk with people about their rights, we come up with a list of all the rights that people think they should have. Then I ask them what they think the other part of rights is. Sometimes they know, but sometimes they don't. If they don't know, I point out that they are adults, and I ask them how adults are supposed to act; when they say "responsible," I try to help them see the connection between being responsible adults and having responsibility for their actions. That's what People First is about.

Keith: Rights and responsibilities are critical issues, but I am sure that there is more to your work than simply pointing out that individuals have rights and responsibilities. What other kinds of things do you do in workshops and meetings with persons with disabilities? What other activities are necessary to help people improve their own quality of life?

Ward: I also help people learn how to start chapters of People First. There are four things that I think you need to have to start a chapter.

First, I think it's real important that local people with disabilities really want it. We sometimes get used to tokenism, because it looks good for local services to have a chapter of People First. But people with disabilities need to run their own chapters because if we can't manage our own rights and responsibilities in the chapter, how will we learn to be a part of society and to access our own communities?

Second, it's necessary for the chapter to have an advisor to give the People First chapter support. This person should not be paid, because people with disabilities need real friends. They already have enough paid people in their lives.

Third, the advisor should not be an employee of the local service agency. If the advisor works for the service agency, he or she may have a conflict of interest. Suppose, for example, that People First members decide that they don't want to work in a workshop, but that they want real jobs—but the advisor is a supervisor in the workshop. Where will the advisor's loyalty be?

Fourth, the advocacy meetings should not be held in the agency. The kinds of issues that members might bring up might not be comfortable to talk about in front of agency staff. People should be able to talk about anything they want, and there should be a two-way trust between members and the advisor. Meetings could be held in libraries, churches, or any accessible community facility. Many of these meeting places can be arranged for free.

Keith: Clearly, you feel that self-advocacy chapters must maintain some independence from service providers. Yet, there are certainly good people working in the field, people who have been very important to the evolution of self-advocacy. Is there any role that you believe can or should be played by service providers in the self-advocacy movement?

Ward: I am not saying that people who work for service systems are all bad. I just think it's difficult for people to learn to have confidence in themselves when they spend all their time with paid

supervisors. At the same time, staff members may be the only available advisors at first, and a good staff person may need to serve until contact can be made with other community people.

Staff people can also help by teaching members how to get to meetings using public transportation, or by providing transportation, or by helping members learn and remember when meetings are held. They can help people gain confidence in themselves, by giving them more responsibility in their home lives, jobs, and communities.

The last point here is that service providers should listen to people with disabilities, because if we are allowed to come up with ideas and feel that our ideas are being carried out, it will improve our quality of life.

Keith: I know that you have some ideas about the potential role of other community organizations in the lives of people with disabilities. I am thinking, for example, about community service clubs, churches, and other social institutions in the towns and cities where people live. Our research on quality of life has shown us that these are important to the residents of a community.

Ward: When I go to a town and help people start a chapter, I go first to the Chamber of Commerce to get a list of service organizations. Then I help the local people go through the list and come up with ideas for the ones that might help them find an advisor, provide assistance for people with physical disabilities, and arrange transportation. There are a lot of ways for community people to help besides giving money.

This is another place where service providers can help. For example, staff can help people approach the community organizations, and they can give support when members are presenting

7

their needs and asking the community groups for assistance.

Keith: I would like to ask you to return to the self-advocacy advisor for a moment. You have suggested that the advisor should, ideally, not be a staff member of the service provider—that it is more desirable to find an interested, supportive community person. I understand the reasons for this, but I can also imagine that this must mean that it is sometimes important to provide some orientation or training for such individuals. At the least, it would seem important to keep certain characteristics in mind when selecting an advisor.

Ward: The advisor is a very important part of the chapter, because the advisor is the person who will teach the members how to access their community, run their meetings, and all the other things people will want to learn. For example, eventually, the members might want to learn about legislation; there is a lot of legislation that affects people with disabilities, and if we don't learn about that, how will our elected representatives know how we feel?

I think an advisor should be someone who believes in people who have a disability, and is willing to learn from us as well as to teach us, because I also think there are things an advisor needs to learn. For example, they may need to learn when to back off and let us do things on our own and when to kick us in the pants and get us moving.

Keith: One of the most visible functions of People First of Nebraska is the group's annual convention. It has grown over the years, and I know that many of our friends would never miss attending. Can you describe a little of the history and nature of the convention?

Ward: One of the things that People First of Nebraska is most proud of is that

we are self-sufficient. As an organization, it is important for us to be able to say that. Often, the image we have of people with disabilities is that they are constantly given money. We are proud that we do not need lots of outside money to run the organization. People who come to the convention pay their own registration costs and hotel and meals. Income from the registration is the main source of money to support People First of Nebraska.

For the 1994 convention, 404 people registered. At the first convention, 16 years ago, we had about 160. The planning for the convention is done by the board of People First of Nebraska, and it took us a long time to learn how to do that. When we started out, the advisors did everything, but now the board of directors does the whole convention.

This year, we had Hank Bersani from Oregon for our keynote address. He told stories about people who had learned to advocate for themselves, and about why it is important for people with disabilities to be able to do that.

State officers are elected at the convention every two years, and we always have "open mike" time when people can come forward to talk about any ideas they have. They talk about jobs, about closing institutions, what it means to have their own apartments, and things like that. This is how we know what the members want, and it is where People First of Nebraska gets ideas for its goals.

We also have representatives from political campaigns as speakers at the convention. They listen to our concerns about issues like wage-and-hour laws, and they respond to our questions.

I also have to say that we have a lot of fun at the convention. We always have a dance, and many people go to the convention to see friends they haven't seen for a whole year. It's not only a business meeting, but also a social event. In fact, for some people it's only a social event—just like other people at conventions, some folks don't go to the meetings at all! The convention allows the staff who accompany some people to see those people in a whole new light, in a situation where they are doing things on their own.

Keith: You have been working on the problems of advocacy and its contributions to individual rights and personal satisfaction for many years. What can you say about the history of the movement— where it started, and where it is now?

Ward: There are two different organizations I can talk about: People First of Nebraska and the national organization, Self-Advocates Becoming Empowered.

People First of Nebraska was started by a gentleman named Ray Loomis who lived in our state institution. He was told that he wouldn't last long in the community. It was hard for him, so he wanted to start a support group so that people living in the community would have a way of talking about it. He saw the local service system, the Eastern Nebraska Community Office of Retardation (ENCOR) as the first project, giving people support in the community. So he started Project Two, the first self-advocacy chapter in Nebraska, about 20 years ago. It was called Project Two because it went beyond Project One, to let people provide support for themselves. They didn't really realize that they were doing self-advocacy until they saw a film about People First of Oregon. That was the beginning. Now there are 10 chapters plus five affiliate chapters across the State of Nebraska.

Self-Advocates Becoming Empowered is the name of the national self-advocacy organization. In 1989, people met in Atlanta with a dream of starting a national self-advocacy organization. We wanted it to be a grassroots organization, meaning starting from local chapters up, so that everybody would feel a part of it. We felt that there were lots of chapters around the country, but each one didn't know what the others were doing. A national organization would let them communicate with each other.

In 1990 we had our first national conference, in Estes Park, Colorado. We worked on leadership skills and developing a policy statement on how people with disabilities wanted to be treated. After everyone signed it, we sent it to Washington to the President.

The next year, we had our second national conference in Nashville, Tennessee. The national steering committee put together a booklet that had a national definition of self-advocacy, a national belief statement, and the goals of the national organization. The best thing about that is that it was all done by us, and the steering committee and other people with disabilities helped the members who couldn't read to vote. At that conference we also agreed on the nine different regions of the country that make up the organization.

Now there are about 40 states that have some kind of organized self-advocacy movement. The national steering committee is made up of 16 representatives who meet four times a year to run the national organization. One of the exciting things that the organization is doing now is working on closing institutions across the country—and it's being recommended by a group made up of people with disabilities. Another thing we're proud of is the fact that we were the first group made up of people with disabilities to hold a meeting at Wingspread, the international conference center where American Presidents and other important people have held meetings and conferences.

Keith: As you know, we have seen many changes in service programs and philosophies in the past few years, and we are also seeing changes in the willingness of people to support various kinds of human services in our country. In this context, what do you expect to be the future of self-advocacy? What do you think self-advocacy programs will look like as we approach the 21st century?

Ward: I think self-advocacy organizations will become the next ARC (the parents' organization) because now we're starting to speak out for ourselves and becoming stronger by working together to achieve one voice. One way we are learning to speak out for ourselves is by telling other people how we feel about things. That means that we need to be able to make decisions for ourselves and to let people like parents know what we want. We are not saying that they should not help, but that we need to decide the end goal for ourselves, so it's what we want.

By learning how to work together, we are also learning that we can make a difference in politics. If you had all the people with a disability—no matter what type—banded together, you might have a majority, and we could elect our own

political officials. Issues that affect people with a disability would be heard and taken seriously. That is what the future should look like.

Finally, my dream for the future is that I work myself out of a job, because there will be no need to have organizations that work with people who have a disability. People with a disability will be accepted like anybody else, so there won't be a need for those kinds of organizations. That is my dream.

I also know that quality of life is related to being in the community, to personal empowerment, and to the opportunity to make personal evaluations of life experiences. The self-advocacy movement is clearly moving people in these directions, empowering them to evaluate their own experiences and to demand a place in the mainstream of community life. Tom Houlihan stated it eloquently:

> *I believe in peace between people—peace between people who have different thoughts about life. I believe we should try to make each other happy. I think People First can help bring that peace.*
>
> **(William & Shoultz, 1982, p. 43)**

References

Williams, P., & Shoultz, B. (1982). *We can speak for ourselves.* London: Souvenir Press Ltd.

Quality of Life and the Individual's Perspective

Steven J. Taylor and Robert Bogdan

Center on Human Policy
Syracuse University

Quality of life is an elusive concept, especially when applied to people with mental retardation. We do not have an agreed-upon standard for determining anyone's quality of life. In fact, we seldom make inquiries into the quality of life of people who are not disabled or disadvantaged in some way. It is ironic that we usually examine quality of life only when we know or suspect that people are suffering. Herein lies both the importance and danger of studying the quality of life of people with mental retardation.

On the one hand, the concept of quality of life directs attention to the human needs of people who have developmental disabilities. Although it is important that service systems and schools help children and adults with mental retardation to learn and develop, it is more important that they contribute to the quality of life of the people they serve. The strongest indictment of institutions and segregated schools is not that they fail to teach people, although

this case could be made, but that they deny people respect and dignity. The increasing interest in quality of life marks our recognition of the assaults to the dignity of people with mental retardation, very often done in the name of humanity (Blatt, Ozolins, & McNally, 1980).

On the other hand, because we do not ordinarily study the quality of life of nondisabled people, the study of the quality of life of people with mental retardation runs the risk that these people will be singled out further as different from the rest of us or even dehumanized. As the most extreme example of this danger, quality of life has been cited as a justification for euthanasia and withholding medical treatment from infants with severe disabilities (The Association for Persons with Severe Handicaps, 1984; Hentoff, 1985). In an infamous experiment carried out at the University of Oklahoma Health Sciences Center, medical researchers employed a quality of life formula to assist in medical decision-making regarding treatment for infants with spina bifida:

> $QL = NE \times (H + S)$, QL is quality of life, NE represents the patient's natural endowment, both physical and intellectual, H is the contribution from home and family, and S is the contribution from society.
>
> **(Gross, Cox, Tatyrek, Pollay, & Barnes, 1983, p. 456)**

Even when quality of life is not used to justify outright discrimination, formulations of quality of life for people with mental retardation run the risk of applying standards to their lives that nondisabled people would not accept. Although this danger is real, it is not inevitable. The challenge is to study the lives of people who have developmental disabilities in a way that emphasizes our common humanity. This chapter looks at quality of life from the perspective of the individual labeled mentally retarded and argues that the concept of quality of life has no meaning apart from the experience of individuals. Because the focus is on the individual's perspective, we start with the stories of three individuals.

Listening to People's Stories

The following excerpts contain parts of the life histories of three people, Ed, Pattie, and August. The names of Ed and Pattie are pseudonyms; because August was a plaintiff in a lawsuit and his circumstances were made public, his real name is used.

Ed's and Pattie's stories are told in their own words and were constructed from the edited transcripts of in-depth interviews (Taylor & Bogdan, 1984). These excerpts are taken from detailed life histories published elsewhere (Bogdan & Taylor, 1982). Both Ed and Pattie had been labeled mentally retarded, although a reading of their stories calls into question the meaningfulness of the label. In contrast to Ed's and Pattie's stories, the excerpt on August is not presented in his own words and is based on an extensive review of case records and, to a lesser extent, first-hand observations; hence, it is not August's story, but the story of August.

Ed's Story

"What is retardation? It's hard to say. I guess it's having problems thinking. Some people think that you can tell if a person is retarded by looking at them. If you think that way, you don't give people the benefit of the doubt. You judge a person by how they look or how they talk or what the tests show, but you can never really tell what is inside the person.

"Take a couple of friends of mine. Tommy McCan and P. J. Tommy was a guy who was really nice to be with. You could sit down with him and have a nice conversation and enjoy yourself. He was a mongoloid. The trouble was, people couldn't see beyond that. If he didn't look that way it would have been different, but there he was, locked into what the other people thought he was. Now P.J. was really something else. I've watched that guy and I can see in his eyes that he is aware. He knows what's going on. He can only crawl and he doesn't talk, but you don't know what's inside. When I was with him and I touched him, I know that he knows.

"It's a struggle. I'll tell you it's a constant struggle as long as I can remember. You want your brain to function correctly and you try and try. You're at war with your brain. You want your brain to function but you have got to watch it. Like the other day in the cafeteria at work. I took a coffee pot and began walking out of the dining room with it. I was just walking without thinking. I looked down and there it was. I said to myself, 'What the hell are you doing?' and turned around and put it back. Your mind has to keep struggling. You can't give in to that mental-retardation image. You strive to be extra careful. You struggle to be not what the image of the retarded is. You can't look the way they say you are if they call you retarded. Some people can be real smart, but look and act the way a retarded person is supposed to.

"Sometimes being handicapped has its advantages. You can go slower. Living has always been a struggle to get from the bottom to the top—trying to keep up with everybody. I could never get up. There are no short cuts for me—only the hard way. The way I see it now is that the only thing in life isn't just getting up the pole.

"I think I've come a long way, but I've got a way to go. I've gotten to the point where I can accept certain things. Once in a while I go out now and I have a good time—I'll do different things. It's hard though. Like you can't go out and join clubs and things. A lot of ex-residents would like to join the Y. That would be something that I could enjoy. I could go and take a swim. I've had to adjust more to a point where I can just relax. I've learned to relax in certain ways, but in others I haven't. I'm still nervous. There are fears for people coming from a place like Empire [State School].

"What I am basically trying to say is that for the majority of people, a retarded person is someone to be stared at.

You don't want to be seen in a public place. It hurts to watch those people being retarded. And don't talk to anyone unless you know who they are. It's rough and you can't take on the whole world. You try to make the best of your situation and try to think that the world maybe is saying, 'He doesn't look all that retarded.' There are people you just can't talk to. They are responsible if they see it and then make fun of it. People are really ignorant. People consider themselves normal and they put a stigma on people who aren't. They do it out of ignorance. I don't expect people to understand the whole problem. I know that handicapped people are people. They feel and they have a lot to give.

"It is very hard to go through life with a label. You have to fight constantly. 'Retarded' is just a word. We have to separate individuals from the word. We use words like 'retarded' because of habit—just like going shopping every week and getting up in the morning. The word 'retarded' has to be there if you are going to have people help, but what the hell is the sense of calling someone retarded and not giving them anything?

"I don't know. Maybe I used to be retarded. That's what they say anyway. I wish they could see me now. I wonder what they'd say if they could see me holding down a regular job and doing all kinds of things. I bet they wouldn't believe it."

Pattie's Story

"At Empire State School, G Building was for real severely retarded older women. They messed their pants and wet themselves. They would have strings around their fingers and they would whirl the string and look at it. Some of them had bald heads. They would send us over there when we were punished. That was really a sad case when I went over there. They would throw up after they ate and we had to clean it. That was our punishment—cleaning those people in the shower wasn't any fun, either, because they would hit you and pull your hair and stuff.

"I don't know how many times I was sent to G Building. It was quite frequently. The first time I was there I didn't know too much about it. I must have been 12 when I first went on to G. The other girls didn't tell me much. They wanted me to find out for myself, I guess. Once the doctor said that I was going, they didn't waste any time. They sent your papers along with you. The attendant took me down. They said, 'This is Pattie. This is the one that is being punished. Don't give her an easy time. Make her work.' After the first time I was sent there, I started watching other people being punished over there. We would walk through that area when I had to go to church, and I would say 'Hi' to who was there. I would ask how they were and how they were doing. They would be scrubbing floors and I would say, 'You poor girl.' I know because I was there too. I would start crying when everybody went past me when I was there.

"When you were sent to G the only thing you were allowed was what was right there. We were there with the low grades. That's what they called them, 'low grades.' It was another name for severely retarded people. The attendants called them that.

"The first thing they had me do when I first arrived was to clean out the toilets. Then I had to shower some of the girls and dress them. We had to scrub the floors on our hands and knees.

"When I first arrived there and saw all the people, I thought, 'Oh, no. What am I getting into now? What's going to happen?' There are all these people just sitting around and rocking back and

forth and back and forth. Some of them were pulling their hair and eating it. One was in a straitjacket.

"Whenever we had medication they would line us up and they gave it to us down there too. They took us down to the cafeteria with them, and part of the punishment was we had to eat their ground food. They ground your meat and everything. They piled the stuff right up too. That was what they ate, so you had to, too. I got sick and threw up. It was awful, it was nasty-tasting stuff. They asked me what was wrong. I told them that I didn't like it. They told me that I had to eat it because I was being punished. One time the attendant turned her back and I slopped the ground meat into one of the low grade's trays and told her to eat it. I thought that was funny. She just gobbled it right down.

"We had a lot of messers on that ward. Mostly they would do it in their clothes and then we had to clean them. I hated to do that. We had to clean the mess if they went on the floor. I hated it. Who wants to clean someone's rear end at that age? I wouldn't mind cleaning a baby's behind, but not them.

"I started treating them kind of mean because I felt if it wasn't for them I wouldn't be there cleaning them. I would throw them on the toilet. I would say, 'Sit there,' and when I got them in the shower I would turn the cold right on them. Sometimes they would start squealing and the attendant would come running and ask what I was doing. I would say, 'Oh, nothing. She caught her toe in the drain.' I was mad. I said, 'If it wasn't for you I wouldn't be here doing this junk.'

"I didn't think about them low grades being in the same institution as me. I really didn't think about anything. I just knew I was there and I was going to live there for a while. Maybe never get out. I thought I was going to be there until I was in my rocking chair. Maybe die there—but it didn't happen."

The Story of August

I first met August in March, 1979 (Taylor, 1984). He was living then at Craig "developmental center," an institution for the so-called mentally retarded in Sonyea, New York. August had lived at Craig since 1941.

August was one of the most retarded people I had ever met. He couldn't speak, use the toilet, dress himself, or do much of anything. He also had quite a few troubling behaviors. Staff at the institution variously described him as "aggressive," "regressive," the "worst case," and "the most severe behavior problem." He attacked others, resisted directions, and shunned any form of social interaction.

We will probably never know August's side of the story. But the institution's side is well documented in volumes of case records, ward logs, and professional evaluations maintained over the previous 40 years.

Born in New York City in October 1936, August's early years had been far from trouble free. Doctors suspected that he had suffered brain injury at birth, and at 9 months of age he incurred a severe head injury in a fall from his crib. In the fall of 1940, his 26-year-old mother was killed as she attempted to rescue August from the path of an oncoming truck. One year later August, scarcely six now, found himself at what was then Craig State School, hundreds of miles away from his New York City home.

August's first several months at the institution were rather uneventful, at least from the institution's perspective. An entry from the Ward Notes on October 31, 1941, reads: "On ward in good condition. Gets along well with other boys."

By mid-January of 1942, August was striking out at his peers on the ward. "This fellow had been quite well behaved. Lately he attacked other boys who do not fight back." By 1948, he was digging his rectum and smearing feces, and by 1949 he was continually ripping off his clothes.

Throughout the 1950s and '60s, August received a panoply of behavior control drugs: "…he is constantly under heavy sedation." At one time or another, he received Thorazine, Trilafon, Prolixin, Haldol, Quide, Ritalin, Stelazine, Serentil, Dexedrine, Mellaril, Valium, chloryl hydrate, Dalmane, and more. The drugs took their toll. By 1958, August began to experience extrapyramidal disorders, drug-induced pseudo-Parkinson's disease involving twitches, tremors, difficulty ambulating, and loss of balance. To this day, August walks with an unsteady gait.

Yet the drugs did not control his behavior, reduce his aggression, or eliminate his untidy personal habits. The doctors recognized this as early as 1961. But as late as 1979, they continued to prescribe drugs such as Haldol, even though it seemed "to be ineffective as far as controlling extreme aggressive behavior."

August spent the '50s and '60s in restraint: "Has to be in camisole most of the time." "Occasionally, patient has days and short periods of time out of restraint."

By the early 1970s, August had lost weight, looked "emaciated and run down," had become "dull and lethargic" and had begun "falling frequently." He still occasionally assaulted his fellow inmates and staff.

They extracted August's teeth around this time. And he lost one ear to the surgeon's knife. His ear was injured somehow, and he just kept picking at it. The records do not say much more about this. What is it about facilities or programs that we can find out more about a man's bowel habits than how he lost his ear?

Sometime around the spring of 1972, August started living in a shower room on his ward. The records do not say a lot about this either. Three months' worth of ward notes for this period are missing completely.

August spent the next seven years of his life in that shower room. Staff members said they did all they could to coax him out of there. His program plans for the period contain a goal of keeping August out of the shower room.

One staff member recalls that during the three years he worked on the ward, August was locked in the room by the staff. Tears came to this large man's eyes as he described how August did not see the light of day for several long years.

The day I first met August was his second day out of the shower room. August lay on the floor, grunting and groaning, with an agonized look on his face. He did not seem too interested in having visitors—no greeting, no eye contact, no sign of recognition.

As a result of a lawsuit, August was moved out of the institution. The last time I saw him he was living in a house with six other people. The house was located not far from Craig and formerly was the groundkeeper's residence. It was not part of the community, but it was not the institution either.

August spent his days at a Medicaid-funded "day treatment center." He sat at a table sorting blue and yellow pieces of paper, putting pegs in a pegboard. For doing this day in and day out, August got oyster crackers and some kind words.

August was a changed man. I knew this when he reached out his hand to shake mine.

August had developed some skills and never caused any trouble. He was toilet trained, ate with a fork and spoon, and not only kept his clothes on, but dressed himself.

Perhaps the biggest change in August was his sociability. He never used to smile at anyone else. Now he thrived on human contact. This wild man, this aggressive and then asocial individual, spent the better part of an hour holding my hand, patting me on the back, and taking my hand and stroking the side of his head with it. The supervisor of August's home said that everyone liked working with August. She described him as "loving, kind, and gentle."

Quality of Life As Subjective Experience

Quality of life is a matter of subjective experience. The concept has no meaning apart from what a person feels and experiences. It is a question of how people view or what they feel about their lives and situations and not what others attribute to them. Although we may make assumptions about Ed's, Pattie's, and August's quality of life based on where they lived, what is important is how they experienced their lives.

Quality of life refers to one's satisfaction with one's lot in life, an inner sense of contentment or fulfillment with one's experience in the world. As a subjective experience or feeling, quality of life may or may not be something that people think about. It is probably only during the highs and lows in life that anyone devotes much thought to quality of life. In fact, most people would not use the phrase "quality of life" to describe their feelings about their existence.

Factors external to individuals can and do influence their quality of life

(O'Brien, 1987). One can assume that the abusive and dehumanizing conditions described and depicted so vividly in Blatt's institutional exposes (Blatt, 1970; Blatt & Kaplan, 1974; Blatt et al., 1980) produced a miserable quality of life for people confined to those facilities. Pattie's story certainly confirms this. Similarly, one can reasonably assume that caring and loving families create a high quality of life for their members. Yet factors influencing one's feelings and subjective experience should not be confused with those feelings and subjective experience themselves.

What does quality of life mean? Although there are many ways to define and study quality of life, the position taken here is that quality of life must be studied from the perspective of the individual. The following six propositions, which are summarized in Table 2.1, are proposed to guide inquiries into the quality of life of people with mental retardation.

Table 2.1
Propositions to Guide Inquiries Into the Quality of Life of People With Mental Retardation

1. Quality of life may be experienced differently by different people.

2. The study of quality of life requires that labels be set aside.

3. Quality of life inquiry requires a personal perspective.

4. The study of quality of life poses a methodological challenge.

5. Studying quality of life requires in-depth knowledge of the person.

6. Definitions and conceptions of quality of life must respect people's subjective experience.

Quality of Life May Be Experienced Differently by Different People

People may experience the same circumstances differently. What enhances one person's quality of life may detract from another's. Although some circumstances may produce a nearly universal response in human beings—for example, the treatment accorded August, an individual's quality of life cannot be determined *solely* through examination of the conditions of his or her existence.

Considerations of the quality of life of another person are likely to be characterized by ethnocentrism or chauvinism. The stereotype of the European explorer appalled at the "savagery" of the American Indian clearly illustrates this tendency. Even within cultures, it is common for one class or race to question the folkways and hence the quality of life of another. For example, the upper class denigrates the lifestyle and tastes of the working class. Yet who is to say that theater, literature, and opera create a higher quality of life than television and sports?

This is not to suggest that one should not draw on one's own experiences and feelings to understand another person's. In looking at the quality of life of another person, it is useful to ask oneself, "How would I feel if I were in that position?" This question can provide a useful starting point for inquiries into quality of life. For example, in reading August's story, we must ask ourselves what it would feel like to be restrained for years and to be subjected to constant sedation. In order to understand another person's subjective experience, one must be able to empathize with that person without substituting one's own values, beliefs, and interpretations for those of the other.

The Study of Quality of Life Requires That Labels Be Set Aside

The label of mental retardation imposes a barrier to understanding people on their own terms. When a person is labeled "mentally retarded," others are less inclined to take his or her perspective seriously. Burton Blatt used to tell a story about a resident of one of the institutions he and Fred Kaplan visited for their photographic expose of institutions (Blatt & Kaplan, 1974). While Kaplan attempted to take pictures secretly with a camera attached to his belt and hidden by his sports jacket, this resident pointed out the camera to the administrator who was escorting Blatt and Kaplan. The administrator laughed and dismissed the resident, saying, "Boy, these retardates can really have an imagination!" (Bogdan & Taylor, 1982).

Mental retardation is a social construct and metaphor that exists in the minds of people who use it to describe the intellectual states of other people, as Braginsky and Braginsky (1971) write:

> *The term mental retardation is simply a metaphor chosen to connote certain assumed qualities of putative, invisible mental processes. More specifically, it is inferred that it appears as if retarded mental processes underlie particular behaviors. Or, we infer that behavior appears as if it were retarded.*
>
> **(p. 15)**

To characterize mental retardation as a social construct is not to deny differences among people according to intellectual ability or at least certain dimensions of what is referred to as intelligence. It is to suggest that the nature and significance of these differences depend on how they are viewed and interpreted. Just as the existence of people who disturbed or upset others in the Middle Ages does not prove the existence of witches (Szasz, 1970), the existence of people who seem intellectually deficient does not prove the existence of mental retardation.

Labels like mental retardation affect how people are viewed by others. Defining people as mentally retarded does not engender closeness or empathy with them. To the contrary, the label provides a filter through which to interpret what they say and do. It becomes easy to dismiss their perspectives, feelings, and experiences as symptomatic of an underlying pathological state. In August's case, for example, staff interpreted his behavior in terms of profound mental retardation, rather than trying to find out what he was feeling. Whatever utility the label mental retardation may have for administrative or programmatic purposes, it can stand in the way of understanding people on their own terms and studying quality of life as they experience it.

If, as suggested above, quality of life has to do with people's subjective experience, then anything that interferes with grasping that experience must be put aside. The study of the quality of life of people defined as mentally retarded requires that we suspend or bracket assumptions and beliefs about mental retardation.

Quality of Life Inquiry Requires a Personal Perspective

Because quality of life is something that is experienced subjectively by the individual, the individual's perspective or point of view must be the primary focus of any study of quality of life. In order to study quality of life we must strive for what Max Weber (1968) called *verstehen,* understanding on a personal level. That is, we must attempt to create in our minds their feelings and experiences.

Citing William James, Bruyn (1966) makes the distinction between *knowledge of* people and *knowledge about* people: "Knowledge *of* people is personal and social, whereas knowledge about people is intellectual and theoretical" (p. 34). It is important to know about people with mental retardation and their situations, where they live, how they spend their time, how others treat them, what opportunities they have. All of these things can impact on their quality of life. But to study their quality of life requires a knowledge of them: in other words, knowing how they feel and view their circumstances.

The Study of Quality of Life Poses a Methodological Challenge

It is easier to study people's life circumstances than how they feel about them. Knowing what another person means and feels is always problematic (Douglas, 1971; Ferguson, 1994). Even seemingly objective words that people use to describe their experiences can have different meanings. Deutscher (1973), in a book on the discrepancy between what people say and what they do, writes:

> *When an American truck driver complains to the waitress at the diner about his "warm" beer and "cold" soup, the "warm" liquid may have a temperature of 50, while the "cold" one is 75...The standard for the same objects may well vary from culture to culture, from nation to nation, from region to region and, for that matter, within any given social unit—between classes, age groups, sexes, or what have you; what is "cold" soup for an adult may be too "hot" to give a child.*
>
> **(p. 191)**

The study of the perspectives and subjective experiences of people with mental retardation may be especially complex. First of all, it may be difficult to interpret interview data. As indicated by Sigelman et al. (1981), obtaining valid and reliable data from interviews with people who have developmental disabilities may be a challenging task. They report that acquiescence (saying what they think the interviewer wants to hear) is a significant problem. During our interviews with Ed, we often had to ask the same question several times in different ways to find out what he really thought. In short, one cannot ask a person with mental retardation, or perhaps anyone for that matter, "How do you view your quality of life?" and expect to receive a meaningful answer.

Second, many people with mental retardation cannot talk or use words to communicate their feelings. August provides an example. Because their inner states or perspectives are not readily accessible, it has often been assumed that they have no inner states; that is, that they do not have subjective experience.

Whether or not people with severe disabilities who cannot speak experience the world like other people is probably unprovable. However, it is just as reasonable to assume that they have subjective experience as to assume that they do not. Family members and others involved in close relationships with people with severe disabilities often state that they can recognize signs of thinking and feeling in their severely disabled loved ones (Bogdan & Taylor, 1989; Goode, 1980a). They can often talk at length about how individuals with severe disabilities think, like, feel, and so on, based on an interpretation of subtle gestures and signs that may not even be apparent to an outsider.

To understand the subjective experience of people with mental retardation, including those with the most severe disabilities, is a methodological problem and challenge. The issue is not whether people have subjective experience, but how we can learn about that experience.

The Study of Quality of Life Requires In-depth Knowledge of the Person

People who know each other well know how to interpret each other's words and acts. For example, spouses usually know when "yes" means "no" and "no" means "yes."

Because it may be difficult to learn about the subjective experience of people with mental retardation, the study of their quality of life calls for knowing them well enough to make reasonable inferences about what they feel and how they experience their lives. To enter into their worlds may entail repeated open-ended interviews over a period of time, as well as other procedures. We interviewed Ed for approximately 50 hours and Pattie for approximately 25 hours.

August could not tell his own story. Yet to say that August could not talk is not the same as saying that he could not communicate. Although inferences

about the subjective experience of someone who cannot speak or use language must be viewed as tentative, August's behavior seemed to say a lot about how he felt and, hence, his quality of life.

In a study of a young deaf-blind girl with mental retardation, Goode (1980b) describes how he used various techniques to understand and relate to her on her own terms. According to Goode, many of the young girl's behaviors that appeared meaningless at first inspection became understandable and rational when viewed from her perspective.

Definitions and Conceptions of Quality of Life Must Reflect Respect for People's Subjective Experience

It is perhaps most meaningful to think of quality of life as *a sensitizing concept.* Blumer (1969), a sociologist, makes the distinction between *sensitizing concepts* and *definitive concepts:*

I think that thoughtful study shows conclusively that the concepts of our discipline are fundamentally sensitizing instruments. Hence, I call them "sensitizing concepts" and put them in contrast with definitive concepts. A definitive concept refers precisely to what is common in a class of objects, by the aid of a clear definition in terms of attributes or fixed bench marks. This definition, or the bench marks, serve as a means of clearly identifying the individual instance of the class and the make-up of that instance that is covered by the concept. A sensitizing concept lacks the specification of attributes or bench marks and consequently it does not enable the user to move directly to the instance and its relevant content. Instead, it gives the user a general sense of reference and guidance in approaching empirical instances. Whereas definitive concepts provide prescriptions of what to see, sensitizing concepts merely suggest directions along which to look.

(pp. 147-48)

Thus, as a concept, quality of life sensitizes us to look at how people with mental retardation feel about and experience their lives and situations. By contrast, "QOL," the operational definition of quality of life, is a definitive concept. The danger of definitive concepts is that they may become reifications with little relationship to what they are intended to measure (Taylor, 1994).

In conclusion, by listening closely to people's stories and attempting to understand how they experience the world, we learn what quality of life means in human terms. Ed speaks about his struggle "not to give in to that mental retardation image." Pattie recalls childhood memories filled with misery on the back ward of an institution. August seems to tell us about his quality of life through his actions: first his aggressiveness, then his self-isolation, and finally, his kind and gentle way. It is seldom, if ever, easy to understand what any person feels and experiences. But without an understanding of how people with mental retardation view and experience their lives, quality of life becomes at best a hollow concept and at worst a justification for treating them in ways that we ourselves would not like to be treated.

References

The Association for Persons with Severe Handicaps. (1984). *Legal, economic, psychological, and moral considerations on the practice of withholding medical treatment from infants with congenital defects.* Seattle, WA: Author.

Blatt, B. (1970). *Exodus from pandemonium.* Boston: Allyn & Bacon.

Blatt, B., & Kaplan, F. (1974). *Christmas in purgatory.* Syracuse, NY: Human Policy Press.

Blatt, B., Ozolins, A., & McNally, J. (1980). *The family papers: A return to purgatory.* New York: Longman.

Blumer, H. (1969). *Symbolic interactionism: Perspective and method.* Englewood Cliffs, NJ: Prentice-Hall.

Bogdan, R., & Taylor, S.J. (1982). *Inside out: The social meaning of mental retardation.* Toronto: University of Toronto Press.

Bogdan, R., & Taylor, S.J. (1989). Relationships with severely disabled people: The social construction of humanness. *Social Problems, 36,* 135-148.

Braginsky, D., & Braginsky, B. (1971). *Hansels and Gretels.* New York: Holt, Rinehart & Winston.

Bruyn, S.T. (1966). *The human perspective in sociology: The methodology of participant observation.* Englewood Cliffs, NJ: Prentice-Hall.

Deutscher, I. (1973). *What we say/what we do: Sentiments and acts.* Glenview, IL: Scott Foresman.

Douglas, J.D. (1971). *American social order: Social rules in a pluralistic society.* New York: Free Press.

Ferguson, D.L. (1994). Is communication really the point? Some thoughts on interventions and membership. *Mental Retardation, 32,* 7-18.

Goode, D.A. (1980a). Behavior sculpting: Parent-child interactions in families with retarded children. In J. Jacobs (Ed.), *Mental retardation: A phenomenological approach* (pp. 94-118). Springfield, IL: Charles C. Thomas.

Goode, D.A. (1980b). The world of the congenitally deaf-blind: Toward the grounds for achieving human understanding. In J. Jacobs (Ed.), *Mental retardation: A phenomenological approach* (pp. 187-207). Springfield, IL: Charles C. Thomas.

Gross, R.H., Cox, A., Tatyrek, R., Pollay, M., & Barnes, W.A. (1983). Early management and decision-making for the treatment of myelomeningocele. *Pediatrics, 72,* 450-458.

Hentoff, N. (1985). The awful privacy of Baby Doe. *The Atlantic Monthly,* January, 54-62.

O'Brien, J. (1987). A guide to life-style planning: Using the Activities Catalog to integrate services and natural support systems. In B. Wilcox & G.T. Bellamy (Eds.), *A comprehensive guide to the Activities Catalog: An alternative curriculum for youth and adults with severe disabilities* (pp. 175-189). Baltimore: Brookes.

Sigelman, C.K., Schoenrock, C.J., Winer, J.L., Spanhel, C.L., Hromas, S.G., Martin, P.W., Budd, E.C., & Bensberg, G.J. (1981). Issues in interviewing mentally retarded persons: An empirical study. In R.H. Bruininks, C.E. Meyers, B.B. Sigford, & K.C. Lakin (Eds.), *Deinstitutionalization and community adjustment of mentally retarded people* (pp. 114-129). Washington, DC: American Association on Mental Deficiency.

Szasz, T.S. (1970). *The manufacture of madness.* New York: Dell.

Taylor, S.J. (1984). A man named August. *Institutions, Etc., 7*(10), 20-23.

Taylor, S.J. (1994). In support of research on quality of life, but against QOL. In D. Goode (Ed.), *Quality of life for persons with disabilities: International perspectives and issues* (260-265). Cambridge, MA: Brookline Books.

Taylor, S.J., & Bogdan, R. (1984). *Introduction to qualitative research methods: The search for meanings* (2nd ed.). New York: John Wiley.

Weber, M. (1968). *Economy and society.* New York: Bedminster Press.

Quality of Life Across the Life Span

Jack Stark and Earl Faulkner
University of Nebraska Medical Center

The concept of quality of life (QOL) has emerged in the 1990s as a sensitizing concept that affects measurement and service provision. The purpose of this chapter is to investigate the concept of quality of life across a person's life span in order to stress the importance of the individual's perspective and thereby understand the concept better. We approach this task not just as a researcher, service provider, teacher, or parent (or parent surrogate in Faulkner's case), but as a combination of all the above with an expressed experiential bias.

For over two decades, significant changes have occurred in the locus and delivery of services for persons with mental retardation. For example, between the years 1968 and 1989, the population of public institutions for persons with mental retardation decreased from approximately 195,000 to 87,000 and the number of persons with a primary diagnosis of mental retardation in state psychiatric facilities declined from approximately 37,000 to 2,000 (White, Lakin, & Bruininks, 1989). Concurrently, persons living in community-based group homes increased from approximately 40,000 to 125,000 between 1977 and 1988 (Amado, Lakin, & Menke, 1990). This deinstitutionalization movement and the widespread philosophical adoption of normalization (Wolfensberger, 1972) led to dramatic growth in community-based living and work alternatives for persons with mental retardation. Due to the widespread adoption and implementation of these concepts, issues related to the quality of life of persons with mental retardation are being addressed. It has been suggested that quality of life is the foremost issue and guiding principle in the design, delivery, and evaluation of services for persons with mental retardation and their families (Goode, 1988; Schalock, 1990).

In the late 1970s, articles on satisfaction and quality of life (Meyers, 1978) began to appear as large groups of persons with mental retardation entered into the community with an emphasis on personal freedom and individual rights (Scheerenberger, 1977). Roos, Wolfensberger, Dybwad, Menolascino and other pioneering philosophers were emphasizing the concepts of the developmental model, normalization, mainstreaming, and least restrictive environments.

Rowitz (1985) recognized that social support was the issue of the 1980s as community integration was in full swing. Landesman (1986) was one of the first to say, Hey, wait a minute! If we are going to use the new buzz-word 'quality of life' in the 1990s, let's define it, measure it, and determine how to apply it to different individuals at different times in their lives.

As we have both watched my 22-year-old son and others like him grow, we have often asked about their quality of life in dealing with issues that vary according to age, support needs, and life domain areas. As social scientists, we recognize the need to address these issues, and we reject the argument of a vocal minority that because there are no real standards or guidelines in the field, facilities can do whatever they think is best to provide services, seemingly without much consumer input and without regard for self-advocacy. This issue looms as the next decade's debate. Edgerton (1990) argues, and appropriately so, that a person's individual choice should be the guiding principle to enhance the quality of one's own life.

Life-Span Research

Research into the concept of quality of life for persons with mental retardation has generally lagged behind and been influenced by other disciplines. The professional fields of social psychology, life-span psychology, gerontology, and medicine have helped shape this relatively new and increasingly popular interest in quality of life research with persons who are developmentally disabled. Of particular interest in this chapter is the research from life-span psychology. Life-span psychologists have contributed to our overall understanding and development of quality of life measures. The life-span development paradigm was originally proposed by

Baltes and his colleagues at the Center for Psychology and Development in West Germany (Baltes, Cornelius, & Nesselroade, 1978). An important point made by Baltes and his colleagues is that they consider their life-span development paradigm not so much a theory as a heuristic scheme upon which to generate new ideas, and which provides a framework for future theory development such as quality of life measures. They noted that their definition of life span allows for additional adaptations and that these adaptations will vary among researchers, particularly as the concept is approached from different disciplines. Other life-span psychologists, such as Dannefer (1984), Featherman (1983), and Gergen (1980), offer additional insight into this complex concept through the utilization of life-span development, which provides a reference basis and body of research data from which we can now begin the process of investigation and identification of life measures, instruments, and field studies to establish a national impetus to foster meaningful life-styles that we all want for persons with or without mental retardation (Schalock, 1986).

Life-Span Perspective

Developmental Stages

Conceptualizing quality of life across the life span is challenging because we lack an all-inclusive theory of normal development, even before adding the complexity and variation of each individual with mental retardation. It is fairly well accepted (Weisz & Zigler, 1979) that with a few exceptions, persons with identifiable developmental disabilities go through the same sequences of development as those without disability. Although much of the research supports the model of mental retardation as a developmental delay, there is also considerable

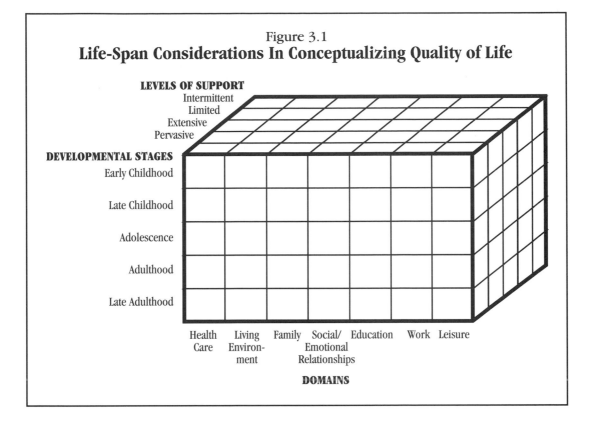

Figure 3.1
Life-Span Considerations In Conceptualizing Quality of Life

evidence indicating that it would be overly simplistic to characterize entirely the development of those with mental retardation as "like normal children only progressing slowly" (Clements, 1988). Individuals with disabilities across the life span may be much more likely to show progression and regression in their development by alternating back and forth between stages of development. That is, they may show far greater discrepancies between levels of functioning in different areas of development even though they may progress through the same sequences in each area. Therefore, there seem to be qualitative differences often based on the cognitive and physical factors of the developmental disability.

Social Systems Theory of Mental Retardation

Pearlin (1980) argued for a social systems theory that stresses the domi-

nant role that community and societal demands and expectations have on adult development. He states that there are many developmental patterns that are shaped by the "confluence of the social characteristics of adults, their standing in the social order, the problematic experiences to which they are embedded, and the coping resources with which they are equipped" (p. 177). The construct of mental retardation within this theory is not viewed as an enduring or continuous trait, but rather exists only to the extent that people label others as having mental retardation. Thus, an individual may be viewed and labeled mentally retarded in one setting or environment, but not in another.

Life-Span Model

Figure 3.1 shows a model for conceptualizing critical variables influencing a person's quality of life across the life

25

span: (a) access to health care, (b) living environment, (c) family involvement and relationships, (d) social/emotional relationships with others (e.g., friends, co-workers, care providers, etc.), (e) education, (f) work environment, and (g) recreation/leisure activity. This model is based on five developmental stages (early childhood, late childhood, adolescence, adulthood, and late adulthood) and four levels of support, ranging from intermittent to pervasive. The levels of support are defined in Table 3.1.

The conceptual framework presented in Figure 3.1 could serve as a basis for conceptualizing variables that potentially impact a person's quality of life throughout life. The model dictates that a certain fluidity and flexibility serve as a fundamental tenet due to the fact that variables are constantly changing. These variables include individual differences, personality characteristics, sociocultural influences, cognitive and adaptive functioning, and etiological considerations.

There are numerous curricula that detail age-appropriate material for services at each of the five developmental stages (Goode, 1988), and there are curriculum materials appropriate for those requiring different levels of support (Steinberg, Ritchey, Pegnatore, Wills, & Hill, 1986). Providing children and adults with age-appropriate experiences and materials is critical to their successful progress in each of these stages, as is adherence to the major principles in the field such as normalization, mainstreaming, inclusion, and self-advocacy. The course of progress across life-span stages is unique for each individual and remains in constant transition throughout the life cycle (Marchetti & Matson, 1988).

Levels of Support

The cornerstone component of all research on the quality of life indicates the importance of support systems in an individual's life. Having someone who cares about and supports each of us is crucial to our daily well-being. Individual supports for persons with mental retardation can be provided by the family, significant others, service providers, or agency personnel (Luckasson et al., 1992). Consistent with the American Association on Mental Retardation's (AAMR) new definition, the old "levels of disability" are replaced by the more accurate way of understanding individual needs, based on the level of intensity of

---

Table 3.1
Levels of Support Intensity

1. **INTERMITTENT**—Supports provided on an *episodic, "as needed" basis.* The individual does not always need the support(s), or needs short-term supports only during life-span transitions (e.g., job loss or acute medical crisis). Intermittent support may be of high or low intensity.

2. **LIMITED**—Supports occurring in some dimension on a *regular basis for a short period of time*—time limited but not of an intermittent nature. May require fewer staff members and less cost than more intensive levels of support (e.g., time-limited employment training or transitional supports during the school to adult provider period).

3. **EXTENSIVE**—Supports characterized by *ongoing, regular involvement* (e.g., daily) in at least some environments (such as work or home) and *not time-limited* (e.g., long-term work support and long-term home living support).

4. **PERVASIVE**—Supports characterized by their *constancy and high intensity.* Supports are provided in several environments and potentially life-sustaining in nature. Pervasive supports typically are *more intrusive* and involve more staff members than do extensive or limited supports.

Note. Adapted from Luckasson et al. (1992), p. 26. Reprinted by permission.

supports needed in order to function optimally. The need for support (as summarized in Table 3.1, Luckasson et al., 1992) can vary across the life span and across the various domains. For example, an individual who has significant medical needs may require a pervasive level of support in the health domain, yet require only limited support in the leisure area. It is important to survey the person directly or via significant others in their environment to determine if each domain is being properly addressed in order to improve quality of life with the various kinds and intensities of support needed across the life span.

Quality of Life Domains

For purposes of this chapter, seven quality of life domains are proposed. There could well be more depending on how specific one wants to be. It is important to note, however, that the 10 adaptive skill areas used in the 1992 definition of mental retardation (Luckasson et al., 1992) are included in these seven domains, with numerous skill areas such as communication, self-care, self-direction, and community use addressed under the education domain. Each of the domains will require continuous monitoring and upgrading in the delivery of services to correspond to changes in the individual's age and levels of needed support.

Health Care

Recently, the health care crisis has received unprecedented attention, as the delivery of health care services now well exceeds 10% of our gross national product. This alarming growth has brought about tremendous changes, particularly the use of managed care. These changes, along with the aging of our overall population, including people with mental retardation, are causing a

great deal of concern among our professional organizations and the state and local programs responsible for directing and funding medical care for persons with mental retardation. It is absolutely essential that all individuals with mental retardation have access to high-quality, primary-care physicians and the ability to receive referrals to specialists as their cases dictate. Potential reductions in Medicare and Medicaid with the emphasis on holding down the costs by using health maintenance organizations will require a great deal of our attention, particularly over the next 10 years, as health care in this country undergoes changes that were unthinkable just five years ago.

There are approximately 100,000 people still residing in public residential facilities, many of whom are on medication, particularly those who are classified as elderly, medically fragile, and those with various psychiatric disorders. Many of them have complex medical and psychiatric needs and require special resources in order to move into community settings, particularly in sparsely populated areas (Buehler, Menolascino, & Stark, 1986). Chronic problems among this population (more than 40% are affected) continue to be much higher than in the general population, particularly with seizure and psychiatric disorders that require careful monitoring, medications, and access to specialists in neurology and psychiatry. On a more positive note, however, we continue to see growth in the number of physicians throughout the country who seem genuinely interested in providing services to our clients.

Living Environment

No other area or domain has perhaps received as much attention as living environment has as the main quality of life indicator. Many consider a person's living environment to be the most important domain because it provides a major influence on social and emotional development (Rutter, 1985). Research by Lehman, Slaughter, and Meyers (1991) supports the hypothesis that a quality of life gradient exists across living settings for individuals with psychiatric and cognitive disabilities, ranging from a lower quality of life in large facilities to higher quality of life scores in small community or home settings.

Most younger persons with disabilities today remain in the family home until young adulthood. Those who need an intensive support system may need specialized types of residential care in the community after leaving the school system. For example, Meyers, Borthwick, and Eyman (1985) examined different types of residential settings in a survey of some 60,000 persons with developmental disabilities in California. These investigators found that of all the people surveyed (birth to 65 years of age), 63% continued to live at home, 29% lived in community settings, 13% in institutions, and 5% in health facilities. The majority of younger individuals lived at home and, as they entered the 25-30 years age-range, over 50% moved outside of the parents' home.

Family

The frequency, intensity, and emotional support level of intimacy depends on the family. It is crucial in the development of a person with mental retardation, particularly early in the life span, to have as much family support as possible. The family life-cycle theory advocated by the Turnbulls has significant implications for persons with disabilities and their families. The Turnbulls have provided a framework in which the uniqueness of each family, the role of each family member, and the development of short- and long-term goals for each individual

with disabilities can be considered (Turnbull, Bronicki, Summers, & Gordon, 1989).

Social and Emotional Relationships

Quality of life is significantly impacted by the caring and bonding of caregivers, peers, and friends in the social and emotional context in which we spend our days, whether this be at school, work, or home. The home/school systems, vocational agencies, and community programs are the primary social agents responsible for providing each individual a smooth transition from one life stage to another. Social adjustment scales have been developed to inform decisions about the appropriateness of independent living options and sexual and emotional relationships. Providing life-style support is an important role for service providers at each of the developmental periods (Newton, Horner, LaBaron, & Sappington, 1994). Longitudinal research on the quality of life of individuals (see Edgerton, this volume) provides us with evidence that people are willing to sacrifice a great deal to maintain their own autonomy and friendships, even residential comforts.

Education

Special education programs in this country are being challenged to do more with less and are in a "quality" crisis. For the first time since 1973 and the implementation of Public Law 94-142, individuals are graduating from our school systems having benefitted fully from special education services. These programs have been successful in identifying, evaluating, classifying, and placing students into classes with curriculum programs designed to meet individual needs.

The really disappointing and frustrating outcome, despite these Herculean efforts, is that students have no programs or services after school, and they go on waiting lists and reside at home. We have been unable to transition this population into the mainstream of society. Of the approximately 700,000 special education students graduating each year, including students with mental retardation, only one-fifth find full employment, and half of them are underemployed (U.S. Department of Education, 1991). People with mental retardation are often relegated to day programs and sheltered workshops.

A funding crisis is threatening to do even more harm to the quality of special education services. Special education enrollment continues to grow faster than total enrollment, particularly in suburban settings. Ninety percent of the costs of special education is provided by the states, which have 10 to 15% of their total school population in special education classes. However, special education costs have been going up an average of 10% a year over the last 10 years, prompting a call for a cap in many states. This changing phenomenon will require more work at the state level to introduce innovative programs emphasizing quality of life concepts in educational programs given these restraints (Isaacs, Percival, Gombay, & Perlimann, 1994). In addition, the increase in drug and alcohol related births, survival of primitive infants, and the ongoing family unit breakdown are also complicating special education efforts.

Work

The American work force is undergoing unprecedented changes due to cutbacks, mergers, and automation, resulting in less need for minimally skilled workers and more high tech jobs. This condition has resulted in underemployment and virtual elimination of middle-income skilled craftsmen, all of which is having profound implications for persons with disabilities. In the 1970s we witnessed the development of sheltered workshops, which emphasized contracts with industry. The 1980s brought employment opportunities in sheltered enclaves and direct competitive placement opportunities, particularly in the service industries. The supportive employment concept has dominated the 1990s and has infiltrated the vocational rehabilitation systems, particularly for the more severely disabled. National survey data by Schalock, McGaughey, and Kiernan (1989) found that facilities providing vocational services to adults with developmental disabilities still employ the majority of individuals in sheltered environments, with approximately 20% in nonsheltered job placements involving food services, building services, and assembly occupations.

Traditionally, the attitude towards work has been that it provides important meaning to a person and helps define who one is and how one can contribute. It has been our experience that persons with developmental disabilities do indeed want to work if they are not relegated to low paying, menial, boring jobs. Some advocates now believe that persons with mental retardation have the right to work in the community in jobs that are meaningful and pay regular wages. Our concern is that those who are left behind in the sheltered workshops are being viewed as unemployable by the vocational systems. Some have argued that persons with mental retardation have a right not to work but should have an opportunity to explore other opportunities. Overall, the research literature favors work opportunities because work strengthens social networks and improves dignity and self-esteem (Ochocka, Roth, & Lord, 1994).

Leisure

Traditionally, recreational opportunities and leisure experiences have been given a low priority in educational and adult programming of citizens with mental retardation. However, society seems now to be moving towards an understanding that if people are to have quality in life, they need leisure experiences that help promote a healthy lifestyle (Dattilo & Schleiens, 1994). One client that we recently worked with, who has had two limbs amputated, perhaps best summarized this philosophy when he stated, "I don't live to work, I work to live." Fortunately, our society seems to be moving towards a stronger leisure ethic. Today, recreation and leisure activities are viewed as opportunities to integrate individuals into the community and to cope better with the many stresses in life. It has been pointed out that one of the greatest challenges facing adults with mental retardation is to avoid isolation and loneliness, and that positive leisure experiences contribute to a sense of self-sufficiency as well as empowerment. Of all the domains, the professional community seems to be giving much more emphasis to leisure activities as an intricate part of ensuring life-long quality of living (Fine, 1994).

Conclusion

Recently, the concept of quality of life has emerged as a philosophical and theoretical movement that can well dominate the years ahead. We have been able to define the concept of quality of life, as well as when, where, and why, and most importantly, how to apply it in various settings. We understand better the process and content that make a life of quality. We understand better the theoretical components of quality of life and have formulated recommendations on how to apply this new emphasis in the field in a practical manner so as to improve the total well-being of persons with mental retardation. What we now need to do is to collect additional data and evaluate in a creative fashion whether and how this emphasis on quality of life has improved life for persons with mental retardation. It is hard to argue with the quality of life movement, but we should keep in mind that "getting something done is an accomplishment; getting something done right is an achievement."

References

Amado, A.M., Lakin, K.C., & Menke, J.M. (1990). *Chartbook: Services for people with developmental disabilities.* Minneapolis: University of Minnesota Press.

Baltes, P.B., Cornelius, S.W., & Nesselroade, J.R. (1978). Cohort effects in behavioral development: Theoretical and methodological perspectives. In W.A. Collins (Ed.), *Minnesota Symposium on Child Psychology* (pp. 1-63). Hillsdale, NJ: Erlbaum.

Buehler, B., Menolascino, F., & Stark, J. (1986). Medical care of individuals with developmental disabilities: Future implications. In W.E. Kiernan & J.A. Stark (Eds.), *Pathways to employment for adults with developmental disabilities.* Baltimore: Brookes.

Clements, J. (1988). Early childhood. In J. Matson & A. Marchetti (Eds.), *Developmental disabilities: Lifespan perspective.* New York: Grune & Stratton.

Dannefer, D. (1984). Adult development and social theory: A paradigmatic reappraisal. *American Sociological Review, 49,* 100-116.

Dattilo, J., & Schleiens, S. (1994). Understanding leisure services for individuals with mental retardation. *Mental Retardation, 32,* 53-59.

Edgerton, R. (1990). Quality of life from a longitudinal research perspective. In R. Schalock (Ed.), *Quality of life: Perspectives and issues* (pp. 149-160). Washington, DC: American Association on Mental Retardation.

Featherman, D.L. (1983). The life-span perspective in social research. In P.B. Baltes & O.G. Brim, Jr. (Eds.), *Lifespan development and behavior, Vol. 5* (pp. 1-59). New York: Academic Press.

Fine, A. (1994). Life, liberty and choices: A commentary of leisure values in life. *Journal of Developmental Disabilities, 3*(1), 16-28.

Gergen, K.J. (1980). The emerging crisis in life-span development theory. In P.B. Baltes & O.G. Brim, Jr. (Eds.), *Life-span development and behavior, Vol. 3* (pp. 32-63). NY: Academic Press.

Goode, D. (1988). *Discussing quality of life: The process and findings of the work group on quality of life for persons with disabilities.* Valhalla, NY: Mental Retardation Institute, Westchester, County Medical Center.

Isaacs, B., Percival, S., Gombay, B., & Perlimann (1994). Social context for understanding the quality of life. *Journal on Developmental Disabilities, 3*(2), 45-58.

Landesman, S. (1986). Quality of life and personal life satisfaction: Definition and measurement issues. *Mental Retardation, 24,* 141-143.

Lehman, B., Slaughter, J., & Meyers, C. (1991). Quality of life in alternative residential settings. *Psychiatric Quarterly, 62*(1), 35-39.

Luckasson, R., Coulter, D., Polloway, E., Reiss, S., Schalock, R., Snell, M., Spitalnik, D., & Stark, J. (1992). *Mental retardation: Definition, classification, and systems of supports.* Washington, DC: American Association on Mental Retardation.

Marchetti, A., & Matson, J. (1988). An introduction to developmental disabilities: A life-span perspective. In J. Matson & A. Marchetti (Eds.), *Developmental disabilities: A life-span perspective.* Philadelphia: Grune and Stratton.

Meyers, C.E. (Ed.). (1978). *Quality of life in severely and profoundly mentally retarded people: Research foundations for improvement.* Washington, DC: American Association on Mental Retardation.

Meyers, C.E., Borthwick, S.A., & Eyman, R.K. (1985). Place of residence by age, ethnicity, and level of retardation in mentally retarded/developmentally disabled population in California. *American Journal of Mental Deficiency, 90,* 266-270.

Newton, J., Horner, R., LaBaron, B., & Sappington, G. (1994). Conceptual amount of improvement in social life with individuals with mental retardation. *Mental Retardation, 32,* 393-402.

Ochocka, J., Roth, D., & Lord, J. (1994). Workplaces that work successful employment for people with disabilities. *Journal on Developmental Disabilities, 3,* 29-51.

Pearlin, L.I. (1980). Life strains and psychological distress among adults. In N.J. Smelsor & E.H. Erickson (Eds.), *Themes of work and love in adulthood* (p. 174-192). Cambridge, MA: Harvard University Press.

Rowitz, L. (1985). Social support: The issue for the 1980s. *Mental Retardation, 23,* 165-167.

Rutter, M. (1985). Family and school influences on cognitive development. *Journal of Child Psychology and Psychiatry, 26,* 683-704.

Schalock, R. (1986, May). *Current approaches to quality of life assessment.* Paper presented at the Annual Meeting of the American Association on Mental Retardation, Denver, Colorado.

Schalock, R.L. (Ed.). (1990). *Quality of life: Perspectives and issues.* Washington, DC: American Association on Mental Retardation.

Schalock, R.L., McGaughey, M.J., & Kiernan, W.E. (1989). Placement into non-sheltered employment: Findings from national employment surveys. *American Journal of Mental Retardation, 94,* 80-87.

Scheerenberger, R.C. (1977). Community settings for mentally retarded persons: Satisfaction and activities. *Mental Retardation, 15,* 3-7.

Steinberg, L., Ritchey, H., Pegnatore, L., Wills, L., & Hill, C. (1986). *A curriculum for profoundly handicapped students.* Rockville, MD: Aspen.

Turnbull, H.R., III, Turnbull, A., Bronicki, G., Summers, J., & Gordon, C. (1989). *Disability in the family: Guide to decisions for adulthood.* Baltimore: Brookes.

U.S. Department of Education. (1991). *To assure the free appropriate public education of all handicapped children: Thirteenth annual report of Congress on the implementation of the Education of All Handicapped Act.* Washington, DC: U.S. Department of Education, Office of Special Education and Rehabilitative Services.

Weisz, J., & Zigler, E. (1979). Cognitive development in retarded and nonretarded persons: Piagetian test of a similar sequence hypothesis. *Psychological Bulletin, 86,* 831-851.

White, C.C., Lakin, K.C., & Bruininks, R.H. (1989). *Persons with mental retardation in state operated residential facilities: Year ending June 30, 1988 with longitudinal trends from 1950 to 1988.* Minneapolis: University of Minnesota, Minnesota University Affiliated Program.

Wolfensberger, W. (1972). *Normalization: The principles of normalization in human services.* Toronto: National Institute on Mental Retardation.

Quality:
A Parent's Perspective

Cathy Ficker Terrill

Ray Graham Association

Our society has evolved into one that is concerned with high technology, high efficiency, and rapid acceleration. These concepts drive our definition and perception of quality in everyday life. However, as we work together to define quality indicators for persons with disabilities, it is critical that we begin by asking people with disabilities and their families for input.

This is the microwave era of society. I come home and open, close, and zap food. If this process takes more than eight minutes, I believe that I have engaged in extensive cooking time and meal preparation. I go to Burger King and have it my way. With their new table service, I can have a sit-down dinner with a baked potato delivered to my table in less than four minutes. If I wait at the McDonald's counter for more than two minutes, I think that the service is slow and thus reflects poor quality management.

Our society is evolving and changing. Technology is altering customers' perceptions of time. What is fast? Is fast quality? Remember when our mail was fast? Now we have fax. We are moving in new dimensions of time and service delivery.

I often visit the library and request books that are already checked out. Staff instruct me to fill out a postcard and guarantee that within three weeks I will be notified in my home that the resource is available. People with disabilities go to providers or the government and request services. Often they are told that there is a long waiting list or that the wait is so extensive, a list is no longer maintained. Think of the customer's perception. Aren't you efficient? How long will the wait be? Days? Weeks? Months? Years?

Burger King can do it my way. McDonald's can deliver in two minutes. The public library can get any book in three weeks. Home health can have a registered nurse in my home within 24 hours. A specialty restaurant can deliver a gourmet meal in less than 30 minutes. The paramedics can respond within three minutes. The American public has become used to and expects customized services within a clearly defined time frame. Yet when a six-month-old child with significant delays needs early intervention, or a family in crisis needs respite, or a young adult graduating from high school needs a job coach, they are often told that there are no resources. As customers in human services, they feel frustrated.

I would like human services to redesign themselves to offer me quality by providing the flexibility of Wendy's salad bar. Think about it.

- Multiple choices

- Everything from spinach to chocolate pudding

- A sneeze guard for safety

- Return multiple times for one price

- Selections change with people's preferences

- All the pieces are out in full view to allow informed choices

- Fixed price not based on utilization

- If I want more, I can go back

Quality in human services should be based on informed choices, multiple selections, and be customer responsive. However, in many communities there is only one option. There is this bed or take this slot. As customers define quality, professionals will be asked to deliver flexibility, alternative supports, creative options, and customized services. The definition of quality will come from the marketplace.

Services from traditional providers have not always been modeled with market driven supports like the use of high technology, customized services, and multiple options. Social service and government agencies don't deliver like McDonald's or the Marriott Corporation. We are not always courteous to customers, and we don't respond with flexible options to meet needs that are culturally sensitive.

Karl Albrecht (1993) addresses the problems of applying total quality management (TQM) to a service industry. TQM focuses on numbers, work process, and management. Albrecht argues that a direct application of total quality management could be nearsighted. The approach he recommends is to take a long view and focus on the reason for the social service organization's existence, which is to serve. Take this a step further: The purpose is to empower, that is, to provide the skills, tools, and supports necessary for inclusion and interdependence.

Albrecht defines quality as a measure of the extent to which a thing or experience meets a need, solves a problem, or adds value for someone. Total Quality Service is a mechanism by which an organization delivers superior value to its stakeholders: its customers, its board, and its employees.

Social service organizations that intend to be the leaders of the future should look at options that meet customers' needs. According to Albrecht, a customer-based strategy must include the following elements:

- a clear corporate mission and guiding principles based on customer need

- a well-defined customer package designed to promote total quality as perceived by the customer

- a system for managing the delivery of the customer package to ensure a high-value experience for the customer

- a statement of goals and objectives that can drive the quality initiative

Quality enhancement involves restructuring business to be person focused, mission and policy directed, and outcome oriented. Sue Gant (1990) acknowledges the challenge of balancing the regulating and enhancing methods of quality assurance systems. She says that "the real challenge is in balancing the design of the system so that the system protects individuals who are seen as vulnerable and in need of support, while at the same time designing strategies that empower individuals to speak out and participate in the review of their system of service delivery" (p. 317). This results in a conflict in the definition of quality. On the one hand, providers want to protect people with disabilities; on the other, to empower them to reach their goals for the future.

Quality of Life Indicators

The components of quality service are many, yet they are all equally important. Let me distinguish between a service and a support. A service is something I obtain from a community vendor, often at a clinic, hospital, dentist's office, or mental health center. A support is something that improves the quality of my life in my home. The following quality indicators, which are summarized in Table 4.1, define quality for my family.

Table 4.1
Key Quality Indicators From a Parent's Perspective

Location

Community Participation

Choices

Safety

Control of Finances

Health

Location

Early intervention and respite should be delivered in a natural setting because, I believe, they are family supports. A natural setting for young infants and children is their foster, adopted, or natural home. My definition of quality is influenced by whether our family is supported in our home to have a better quality of life, or whether I must go forth and use a service in a center-based program that may or may not have similar tools for replication in my home.

Community Participation

Interdependence of community members is a key component of quality. Friendships, neighbors, and family members provide supports, innovative options, and flexibility. The measure is the more people you have in your life who touch you during any given day and are not paid to do so, the higher the quality of life. I couldn't imagine sending my child to a residential facility where the majority of people who have contact with her on any day were paid to do so. Was that a hug or was that a paid embrace? Are you my friend or my paid staff? Friendships can last a lifetime. All children need to learn how to begin and maintain friendships. When children learn to interact with diversity at a young age, we are laying the foundation for future generations.

Choices

Everyone has capacity for choice. It is important that we concern ourselves with the quality as well as the quantity of choices in our lives. Quality supports enhance people's ability to make choices as well as increase opportunities for making informed choices.

As young adults begin to make choices, the process of learning to make informed choices is as important as the choice itself. Many of us take for granted the choices that we have available to us throughout the course of a day. Before I even reach my first destination for the day, I have involved myself in choices relating to food, clothing, hygiene, music, and transportation. I will never forget a young man that I worked with who had left a state institution to live in a home. I asked him what was the greatest thing about his new home. I thought he would mention all kinds of global philosophical things. Instead his thoughtful response was, "The best thing so far is that I get to put cream in my coffee and ketchup on my food." For him, these were new and important choices in his life.

Safety

Life is full of risks. Some are harmful and others are not. If you eliminate risk, you also eliminate a lot of choices or options. Supports and support staff need to be concerned that educational opportunities include opportunities for people to be safe. All of us are exposed to a reasonable amount of risk on a daily basis. To eliminate all risk would result in overprotection and unnatural settings. It is our challenge to allow learning to occur through regular life experiences that vary in the amount of risk involved.

Control of Finances

Unless we decide to join a socialist society, none of us is guaranteed economic security. However, we all need to know what our budget looks like, whether it is a full-fledged budget for an adult or an allowance for a child. It is important to know that we have some control over expenses and income. Because all people have employment potential, managing income is a concept that is important at all ages. Children and adults should have control over their resources. For some people, that is control over their spending money; for others, it means control over their salary; and for others, it means control over their government-sponsored benefits in the form of futures planning.

Health

People often say, "At least I have my health." It is an American indicator of quality of life. Good health includes dental, physical, and mental health. It goes beyond an annual assessment by a medical practitioner to include a comprehensive diet and regular exercise. It allows for good oral hygiene daily, as well as regular check-ups. Good health allows for normal release of frustration, anger, and some healthy laughter.

As we work together to define quality indicators, it is critical that we begin by asking people with disabilities and families for their input. This input must be gathered on the front end rather than as an afterthought. Professionally-driven quality indicators look different from consumer-driven quality indicators. Both perspectives are important to consider. Compare the difference of consumer-directed quality indicators now available through The Accreditation Council and other accreditation standards: the focus has shifted to quality indicators and quality of life oriented outcomes because of input from the customers. As Tom Peters (1987) says, "Quality is about the customer's perception of excellence."

References

Albrecht, K. (1993). *The only thing that matters: Bring the power of the customer into the center of your business.* New York: Warner Books.

Gant, S.A. (1990). The Connecticut model. In V.J. Bradley & H.A. Bersani (Eds.), *Quality assurance for individuals with developmental disabilities: It's everybody's business* (pp. 301-322). Baltimore: Brookes.

Peters, T. (1987). *Thriving on chaos: Handbook for a management revolution.* New York: Harper and Row.

CHAPTER 5

A Grandparent's Perspective: A Special Relationship

Charles A. Gardner

Hastings College

Discussing quality of life as a sensitizing concept requires listening to families and family experiences. For example, when Pete came through the kitchen door that cold December morning in 1984 we knew before he said a word that something was wrong. His face said it all. Much earlier that morning he and his wife, our daughter Kathy, came by to leave their two-year-old son, Alex, with us on the way to the hospital for the birth of their second child. The fact that her labor had begun six weeks early disturbed us all but didn't alarm us. Perhaps it was false labor. Perhaps they and the doctor had miscounted the weeks. Everything would be all right, we thought. But it was not. Pete sat down and said, "Kathy's O.K., but there is something very wrong with our new baby daughter. The doctors don't know what yet."

Although this was our fourth experience becoming grandparents, our expectations, excitement, and anticipated joy were just as high as they had been for each of the previous three. The news that our new granddaughter was born with serious problems and was fighting for her life hit us like a sledge hammer. Our first reactions to the news were a mixture of shock, disbelief, wild hope that things would correct themselves, and sorrow. Over the next few desperate days and weeks we were to experience all the emotions researchers have reported grandparents go through in coming to terms with the new reality of the birth of a handicapped grandchild: shock, disbelief, denial, anger, continuing aching sadness, and finally, acceptance (George, 1988; McPhee, 1982; Murphy, 1990; Seligman, 1991; Vadasy, 1986).

Kathy knew immediately as the child was removed from her womb by caesarian section that there was trouble when the obstetrician quietly exclaimed, "Oh, shit!" and the mood and the activity in the delivery room changed abruptly. Within hours all the tests performed on newborns confirmed that a badly damaged baby had been born. It would be a day or two before more specific medical evidence would confirm that Laura, our new grandchild, had been born with serious and probably permanent neurological damage. None of us in the family had even heard the abbreviation CMV or the term cytomegalovirus, for which the initials stood, let alone its meaning. In the next few weeks we would learn all about it. CMV, a strain of herpes virus, is present in the form of antibodies in 80 percent of adults from infection sometime in their lives. For those minority of women who have not at some time before pregnancy been infected by CMV and thus have not built up resistant antibodies, infection during pregnancy can be, and usually is, transmitted to the fetus. Fetal infection leads to one or more of a panorama of birth defects, including severe mental retardation, blindness, deafness or hearing impairment, and a variety of neurological-muscular impairments. A pediatric physician present at Laura's birth suspected CMV. Tests conducted at a regional medical center confirmed his suspicions. Laura was a CMV baby.

It would be months and countless tests and examinations later before the family would know the kinds and degree of severity of Laura's problems. Although deafness was suspected, brain wave tests later were to prove that she had some hearing in her left ear, although how much was (and still is) unknown. What finally became clear was that she had cerebral palsy which affected her right side severely and especially her throat area, making it impossible for her to swallow correctly or, as it turned out, to articulate speech.

During all of the sorting out process of Laura's physical problems, we in the family struggled through personal sorting out processes of our own. Much has been written about the variety of impacts the birth of a handicapped child has on the parents. But what of the grandparents? How are they affected and how is the quality of life of the handicapped grandchild, the parent-grandparent relationship, and the extended family structure affected by this event? A review of the literature reflects a much smaller

but growing interest in recent years in research about grandparents of children with handicaps. The intent of this chapter is to compare our personal experiences as grandparents with what is reported in the research literature. (I say "our" although Laura's maternal grandmother passed away after a two-year illness in 1993, three months after Laura's eighth birthday. So, much of what I write comes from a grandfather's perspective, and the literature is almost silent about grandfather-handicapped grandchild relationships. Much more has been written about grandmother relationships.)

After the initial shock wears off grief settles in. McPhee (1982) writes that a grandchild "is the link from our past to our future...What happens when this link, this delight, this claim to immortality is born less than perfect?" (pp. 13-14). She answers that grandparents experience a mixture of shock, guilt, anger, and hostility before they come, sooner or later, to accept the new grandchild for what he or she is, not what the child might have been. On the heels of initial reactions comes grief. The grief that we grandparents experience is aptly described by Seligman (1991) who speculates that "grandparents experience a mourning period regarding the loss of the idealized grandchild similar to that which parents of the child must undergo" (p. 3). Murphy (1990), writing about grandparents, warns that "we must grieve in order to heal...Not allowing oneself to feel these tremendous pangs can often result later on in serious depression, stress-related physical illness, insomnia and other emotional problems" (p. 3).

Of course, a grandparent's grief is a double grief. Grandparents grieve for the handicapped child and the life she must face and also for the parents of the child who must bear the countless burdens associated with the rearing of that child. We felt this double grief keenly. We were initially burdened with sadness as we contemplated our loss of a "perfect" grandchild and wondered what Laura's future would be. But we also ached deeply for our daughter and her husband. As Click (1986) so poignantly says:"Your adult child experiences tragedy or loss and your heart aches with the knowledge of your own impotence and how you yearn to go back to the days when a Band-Aid and kiss could fix anything" (p. 3). This double grief experience is commented upon by many writers, including Fewell and Vadasy (1986), George (1988), Murphy (1990), and Vadasy (1986).

But as researchers at the Seattle workshop for grandparents of handicapped children verified, although grandparents reported varying degrees of sorrow, shock, anger, and continuing sadness, the large majority also reported coming finally to acceptance (Vadasy, 1986). In our own situation we experienced all of the emotions (except anger) reported by Vadasy to different extents and at varying times. But we came rather quickly to an acceptance of Laura's situation. As we worked through our double grief, we at the same time found ourselves coming to terms with new realities and new family tasks of reordering lives and priorities, even before all the pieces of the puzzle of Laura's handicaps were in place.

According to researchers, this does not always happen. Many grandparents have great difficulty coming to terms with the arrival of a handicapped grandchild. When such a child is born into a family the parents come immediately under great stress. Grandparents can add to that stress by their reactions and behavior, or they can help alleviate the situation by responding with understand-

ing, sympathy and sensitivity to the heavy emotional load of the parents. A counselor of parents of handicapped children cautions:

> *Children remain children in the eyes of their parents no matter how old they are. It is equally true that parents remain parents no matter how old the children become. Parents are able to stir up in their adult children the feelings of weakness and vulnerability they experienced when they were children. At times when a couple feels stress, these old memories are more easily aroused...*
>
> **("I Wish Our Parents...", p. 87)**

There are a number of reasons why grandparents are often slow in putting aside their hopes and dreams for the future and their personal disappointment and sorrow in order to deal helpfully with the here and now. Sometimes distance creates a problem. Distant grandparents are sometimes overwhelmed by fears because they are unable to be involved immediately in the day-to-day coping with the event and thus cannot allay their fears by observation and involvement. Distance also affords them few opportunities to get to know their grandchild and thus inhibits effective support to both the child and the parents (Vadasy, 1986). In Laura's case, we, her maternal grandparents, and her paternal grandmother all lived close enough to be engaged in Laura's life and available to her parents whenever we were needed. In addition to whatever benefits this proximity may have had for Laura and her family, it certainly allowed the grandparents to get beyond our initial shock and grief quickly and to avoid the fears distance can cause.

Another cause for grandparental inability to face the reality of the situation in a positive way is lack of knowledge. Grandparents are frequently a problem because they don't understand the seriousness of the handicap. Often they feel that nothing serious is wrong with the child or that the child will "grow out of" the problem (George, 1988). Such attitudes cause grandparents to react with confusion, insensitivity, and fear of hands-on experience. These attitudes, unless corrected, only add to the burdens of parents, who in most cases look for and need, at the very least, their own parents' understanding and sympathy. Seligman (1991) says, in his assessment of grandparent roles, "Grandparents have considerable influence on how parents respond to a disabled child" (p. 150). He warns about the negative effects of lack of understanding: "Many parents of disabled infants must cope with more than the disability itself. They must also be concerned with the reaction of their own parents" (p. 148).

In our situation, we were able to avoid these negative and unrealistic attitudes and were able to deal with Laura's problems in a positive way almost immediately, not because of superior moral character, but because we were fortunate enough to be able to become informed. At the time Laura was born, both of us were on the faculty of a college and thus surrounded by informed professional colleagues in special education, psychology, science, and other disciplines who gave immediately and generously of their professional wisdom and experience. In addition, as the college librarian, I had at my fingertips countless information resources, which I

quickly exploited and have continued to use. Further, we were able to tap a network of human resources within the community from many fields of medicine, education, community agencies, and support groups through our personal and professional friendships and acquaintances. Kathy, Laura's mother, herself is a working professional in the fields of special education and psychology, and her knowledge and professional experience as well as her network of colleagues throughout the state provided to her and to us an enormous reservoir of information, support, and ongoing assistance.

Obviously, most grandparents are not so blessed. For them, becoming helpfully informed and overcoming fears, uncertainties, and misconceptions in order to provide strong and confident support to their children and grandchildren can be a formidable, intimidating task. One important way this task can be addressed is through grandparent support groups. Until very recently support groups for grandparents of children with physical and mental disabilities were hardly mentioned in the literature. George (1988) reported that "grandparents appear to be the traditionally underserved population [by support groups]" (p. 130). This now appears to be changing. Seligman (1991) surveyed a number of successful programs developed to provide grandparent education and support. And Minkler and Roe (1993) in their research on grandmother caregivers of crack cocaine babies, report:

Although accurate numbers are hard to come by, there are an estimated 250 support groups for grandparent caregivers in the United States today. Respite programs for grandparent caregivers, community coalitions, hot lines, and peer training programs are among the other developments that have come into being in the last few years to support grandparent caregivers in their often daunting new role.

(p. 178-179)

Although most support groups are located in metropolitan areas, grandparents can usually find other helpful groups in smaller cities and towns. In almost every community of any size, support groups for parents and family of handicapped children have long existed. Most of these welcome grandparents as members and participants. Where such groups do not exist, grandparents can usually find other grandparents in similar circumstances and form a group. Most support groups have, in fact, developed from such grass roots efforts (Minkler & Roe, 1993).

There is evidence that the involvement of grandparents in primary support of their handicapped grandchildren and the children's parents is growing and will continue to grow. It is important to note that approximately 75% of the elderly in the United States are grandparents. And given current life expectancy, the majority of these will fill their grandparenting roles for 20-30 years (Vadasy, 1986). Sonneck (1986) points out that because people are becoming grandparents younger (on average women at age 50; men at age 52) and living longer, their role as grandparents and the supports they can provide need to be examined. Of additional note, changing lifestyles of young adults have created new roles for many grandparents, not only as sources of support but as primary caregivers. These changing lifestyles include divorce, single-parent homes, teen pregnancy, and near universal female employment.

What kinds of support do grandparents bring in their increasingly visible roles, particularly as these relate to handicapped grandchildren? A number of writers have addressed this question. Vadasy (1986) outlines four basic resources grandparents bring: experience (including coping strategies); time (for errands, child care, shopping, respite); access to sources of various kinds of instrumental support (community groups, church groups, fraternal organizations, volunteer organizations, etc.); and financial resources. Seligman (1991) reports the same resources and adds that grandparents also fill roles as playmates and as therapists following the instructions of health professionals. He notes that "by offering support during the initial diagnostic phase and throughout the child's development, grandparents help children cope with their situation" (p. 150). Sonneck (1986) adds to this list storytelling, conflict mediation, and friendship. Murphy (1990) notes especially the importance of the gifts of time and patience in relieving worn-out parents, as well as performing small and routine tasks that enrich the quality of the grandchild's life.

As Laura's grandparents, we found ourselves involved to varying degrees in all the above support roles. That we were able to contribute in some measure in these various ways was due largely to open and close relationships we have always enjoyed with our children and their families and especially with Laura's family, who live close by. Bowen (1978) states that "one of the most effective automatic mechanisms for reducing the overall level of anxiety in a family is a relatively 'open' relationship in the extended family...The frequency and quality of emotional contact with the extended family will predictably improve the family's level of adjustment and reduce symptoms in the nuclear family" (pp. 537-538). We were convinced that the most helpful resource we brought and which I still try to bring is emotional support and love, made possible by an existing and continuing relationship of openness and trust. Whatever else we have been able to provide in the way of time, respite, child care, or financial assistance has been secondary to and dependent upon the framework of love and emotional support our ongoing relationship affords. Seligman (1991) affirms this resource: "Perhaps the most important support grandparents can extend is emotional support" (p. 150).

I have some idea of the difference our support has made to Laura's parents since her birth, but because she is unable to speak, it is difficult to measure accurately the impact of this support on Laura herself and upon her quality of life. But from all the nonverbal communication she imparts (and we have learned to communicate very well in her short lifetime), it seems that her grandmother, before she died, and I have been able to enrich her life and add another dimension of experience that would not have been possible without our involvement. George (1988) concludes from her research that "an individual's adjustment to an illness or impairment is influenced by the response of relatives and significant others" (p. 370). This, of course, poses a challenge to those involved in her life, because close involvement can provide either positive or negative role model patterns. Involvement in another person's life carries serious responsibility. Laura has her own ways, with hugs, smiles, and giggles, to affirm the positive nature of our relationship.

Those symbols of affection are reward enough for any contributions we

might have made to the quality of her life. But there are others. George (1988) notes that as relatives become more supportive of the parents, the parents feel less isolated in their own adjustment to a child's handicap, and that there is no greater therapy than getting involved. She urges parents not only to find ways to support the parents directly, but also to join advocacy groups, speak to community groups, promote support groups, and volunteer with agencies serving handicapped children. Although I have become involved in these secondary activities only to a modest extent, I can certainly confirm from my own personal experience that creative involvement is great therapy and a sure cure for sadness and self-pity.

As Laura grew from infancy into early childhood, our involvement in her care began to form routines. A remarkable and, in 1987, somewhat experimental surgery (lateral dorsal rhizotomy), greatly relieved the spasticity on her right side. This in turn has allowed her to learn to walk and has given her much greater use of all her limbs. She became much more free to play outside and to be included in activities of other children her age. This increased mobility and her involvement in school activities has required much more taxi service to get her from place to place, and grandparents can be very helpful as drivers.

Each week I take Laura from her third-grade classroom to the physical therapist who has worked with her for years. This eight-mile journey is precious time for me because we have a chance to be alone together without interruption. It's a time to visit, tell jokes, and find out how school is going. It's a time to share my hopes and dreams, my disappointments and sorrows. Although the verbalization is strictly one-way, the communication is definitely two-way. I learned long ago that Laura hears and understands far more than a casual observer would guess. The weekly trips over the past five years have been a time of joyful bonding between Laura and me, and it has given me a meaningful role in her development. As Kennedy (1992) has noted, "The greater the extent of one-on-one contact, the greater the degree of closeness" (p. 92). A bonus is the friendship I have formed with her physical therapist, which permits me to observe, question, and learn about Laura's physical progress and therapy.

This is just one of the meaningful and rewarding experiences an ongoing relationship with a handicapped grandchild affords. As Laura matures, our relationship matures. We have discovered the states of grandparental relationships described by Kahana and Kahana (1970) to be true in our experience. Their research showed that children perceive grandparenthood according to their developmental ability. In early childhood, ages 4-5, children see grandparents in egocentric and concrete terms. Grandparents are persons who do things with them, give them things. As children grow older, grandparents are valued more as teachers and adults; grandparents and grandchildren become more open to giving and receiving as they experience a more complete acceptance of each other. Research affirms that these stages are as true for children with developmental disabilities as with other grandchildren. Sonneck (1986) found much the same stages of development and grandparent relationships in her research.

The question occasionally occurs to me whether Laura really understands the familial meaning of "grandfather." Because we have as yet no verbal feedback from her I have no way of knowing if she is aware that I am a blood relative—her mother's father. Or am I, to her, simply a love-giving, care-giving adult friend? It is

really a moot point. I am delighted by our relationship, however she perceives it, and the quality of life we enjoy.

The question of how to define quality of life between grandparent and grandchild and how it may be measured is addressed by Kennedy (1992). He surveyed a group of young adults to measure their assessment of the relationship with their grandparents as they were growing up. He examined the quality of this relationship by asking five questions:

1. Did you feel close to your grandparent?

2. Did you feel known and understood by your grandparent?

3. Did you know and understand your grandparent?

4. Did your grandparent exercise a positive influence in your life?

5. Did you view the relationship as an authentic friendship, not an association maintained by parents as intermediaries?

These questions seem to come as close as one can in defining quality of life in a grandparent-grandchild relationship, and can, perhaps, be used as a rough measuring stick of that ongoing relationship. With a nonverbal granddaughter, answers to these questions will always be highly subjective for me. But there are certainly nonverbal means, as I have discovered, to assess our relationship, even by Kennedy's measures. It is interesting to note, parenthetically, that "much of the research on grandparents has been done with grandmothers. This deficit, together with the changing concepts of fathering, would encourage further research directed toward the experience of grandfathers" (p. 96). I, for one, would welcome such study.

Laura's brother, Alex, is two years older than she. Her sister, Annie, is two years younger. It is a constant challenge to their parents, who must devote an inordinate amount of time and attention to Laura's needs, to be careful not to fail to provide necessary loving attention and nurture to her brother and sister as well. This challenge is one that grandparents share. Sometimes the best help I can be to Laura's parents is in spending time with, entertaining, and enjoying the company of her brother and sister. At those times when her parents must be away from home on trips with Laura to doctors and distant medical centers, I have the chance quite often to be with my other grandchildren and to be involved in their lives. In so doing, everyone in the family benefits, including Grandpa.

What of Laura's future? Vadasy (1986) cautions that grandparents must accept that the future will be less predictable and more difficult for their own adult child and for the grandchild than they had previously envisioned (p. 42). The unknown is always fearful. The grandparents can ease those fears by helping the parents to plan and prepare for the grandchild's future. The author emphasizes that as grandparents become informed about specific handicaps, child development, educational programs, and life-planning strategies, including information on wills, trusts, group homes, and vocational training programs, fear of the unknown is reduced and they become better equipped to plan for the child's long-range needs.

Many grandparents are in a position to help ease family financial burdens in the present and make financial plans for the grandchild's future. Such gifts and financial planning help ease concern for the future. But grandparents need to be informed and careful in their planning. Murphy (1990) cautions that "in many states, having funds in one's own right disenfranchises the disabled individual from vital services and benefits, including Medicaid, group home living and much more" (p. 6). It is certainly the prudent course to seek advice of attorneys or estate planners before drafting a will, giving sizable gifts, or planning estates. In our own case we discovered that our will gifting certain properties to Laura for her care would jeopardize her access to state services, and we changed our will to avoid that possibility.

The best way to alleviate anxiety about the future is to become involved in the present. This is more difficult a task for parents than it is for grandparents, who are keenly aware of their own limited and shrinking futures. Parents must concern themselves with and make plans for the future of their handicapped child; this is not a primary concern of grandparents. The ability grandparents have acquired of living in the present, forgetting the past, and not worrying about a future we will probably never see, frees us to focus on present needs and opportunities. Such an attitude has enhanced the very special relationship Laura's grandmother, before her death, and I have enjoyed with Laura. Our day by day involvement in her life and that of her family with only secondary concern for next week, next month, or next year has sharpened our focus on present needs and the support we can give to those needs today.

What we have given and what I am attempting to continue to give is basically what any grandparent gives to any grandchild. She is our granddaughter first; our granddaughter with special needs second. We very quickly learned the truth that Murphy (1990) expressed well:

Your handicapped grandchild is first and foremost a child— more like other children than unlike. The needs of a special child differ only in degree, not in kind. Your special grandchild responds to your love, your jokes and games, your abiding affection, exactly like any of your other grandchildren."

(p. 7)

What I have gained as the grandparent of a handicapped child far exceeds what I have given. I have gained a special closeness with Laura's family. I have gained a deeper relationship with my other children and their families as we all share the experience of Laura's family. I have gained a new sensitivity to the needs and concerns of other children with handicaps and their families. I have gained a new appreciation for the talents and dedication of professional caregivers and providers. I have gained an enhanced ability to counsel and console other parents and grandparents who experience the arrival of a handicapped child into their families. Most of all, I have gained a very special friendship with a very special person, and have experienced "the joy and closeness that a child of special needs brings to a family" (Seligman, 1991, p. 151).

References

Bowen, M. (1978). *Family therapy in clinical practice.* New York: Aronson.

Click, J. (1986). Grandparent concerns: Learning to be special. *Sibling Information Newsletter, 5,* 3-4.

Fewell, R.R., & Vadasy, P.F. (1986). A handicapped child in the family. In R.R. Fewell & P.F. Vadasy (Eds.), *Families of handicapped children.* (pp. 3-34). Austin, TX: Pro-Ed.

George, J.D. (1988). Therapeutic intervention for grandparents and extended family of children with developmental delays. *Mental Retardation, 26,* 369-375.

"I wish our parents would help us more": Understanding grandparents of children with disabilities (1988). *Exceptional Parent, 18,* 82-88.

Kahana, B., & Kahana, E. (1970). Grandparenthood from the perspective of the developing grandchild. *Developmental Psychology, 3*(1), 98-105.

Kennedy, G.E. (1992). Quality in grandparent/grandchild relationships. *International Journal of Aging and Human Development, 35*(2), 83-98.

McPhee, N. (1982). A very special magic: A grandparent's delight. *Exceptional Parent, 12*(3), 13-16.

Minkler, M., & Roe, K.M. (1993). *Grandmothers as caregivers: Raising children of the crack cocaine epidemic.* Newbury Park, CA: Sage.

Murphy, L. (1990). Focus on grandparents. *Special Parent/Special Child, 6* (2), 2-7.

Seligman, M. (1991). Grandparents of disabled grandchildren: Hopes, fears, and adaptation. *Families in Society: The Journal of Contemporary Human Services, 72,* 147-152.

Sonneck, I.M. (1986). Grandparents and the extended family of handicapped children. In R.R. Fewell & P.F. Vadasy (Eds.), *Families of handicapped children.* (pp. 99-120). Austin, TX: Pro-Ed.

Vadasy, P.F. (1986). Grandparents of children with special needs: Insights into their experiences and concerns. *Journal of the Division for Early Childhood, 10*(3), 36-44.

Part II

The Measurement of Quality of Life

In this volume, we see that quality of life has at least two functions. As discussed in Part I, it is a sensitizing concept that gives us a sense of direction, reference, and guidance in approaching the issue. That reference point, which indicates the dimensions of value that are important, is the individual and his or her evaluation of life events. Quality of life also serves as a research construct, directing efforts at measuring the core dimensions of a life of quality. As we see in Part II, measuring quality of life requires that we develop operational definitions and models of quality of life, and implement multiple methods for assessing it.

Attempts to measure quality of life do not have a long history, even though since antiquity, people have sought a life of quality. Generally speaking, efforts to measure quality of life have historically focussed on either objective or subjective indicators. Objective indicators refer to external, environmentally-based conditions, such as health, social welfare, friendships, standard of living, education, public safety, housing, neighborhood, and leisure activities. Such indicators are good for measuring the collective quality of community life, but are insufficient for measuring a person's perceived or subjective quality of life. Subjective indicators focus on the person's evaluations of psychological well-being or personal satisfaction, including physical and material well-being, interpersonal relationships, social and community activities, and personal development.

In recent years, we have seen increased efforts in measuring quality of life from the perspective of persons with disabilities, asking people with mental retardation and closely related disabilities what is necessary from their perspective for a life of quality. Answering that question—and the methodological challenges posed by it—is the focus of Part II, which attempts to answer two fundamental questions about the measurement of quality of life. First, what aspects of a person's life should be considered; and second, what procedures or approaches should be used in measurement?

We begin with two chapters that summarize answers to the first question. In both chapters, contributors summarize the empirical work to date on identifying quality of life dimensions. The chapters are built on quality of life models derived from the literature and provide a taxonomy of quality of life dimensions identified to date by researchers. In Chapter 6, Carolyn Hughes and Bogseon Hwang indicate the following most commonly referenced quality of life dimensions:

- Psychological well-being and personal satisfaction

- Social relationships and interaction

- Physical and material well-being (including employment)

- Self-determination, autonomy, and personal choice

- Community living and integration

In Chapter 7, David Felce and Jonathan Perry present confirmation of these dimensions, but aggregate them into objective life conditions, subjective feelings of well-being, and personal values and aspirations. Across these three model components, the authors discuss the key roles that physical well-being, material well-being, social well-being, development and activity, and emotional (psychological) well-being play in our conceptualization and measurement of quality of life.

Quality of life has emerged in recent years as an important international, cross-cultural issue. In discussing the issues and challenges of measuring quality of life across cultures, Ken Keith suggests four important principles. First, culture is a construct involving shared values, beliefs, behaviors, and attitudes. Second, while sensitivity to culture is essential, quality of life assessment must still focus on the individual and on our common humanity. Third, it is important to conduct comparative studies that illuminate key characteristics of cultures and the quality of life of persons within them. And fourth, we must recognize and overcome our propensity to project our own norms on people of other cultures.

The measurement of quality of life presents methodological problems that are best approached through multiple methods. The last three chapters in this section summarize the thoughts and experiences of leaders in the area of quality of life measurement regarding the multiple methods that are available to those interested in measuring a person's perceived quality of life and the cautions that one should take in such measurement. In Chapter 9, Bob Edgerton summarizes his longitudinal, ethnographic approach to measurement that stresses the importance that context and seeing the phenomena only through the subject's eyes play in quality of life assessment. Based on his work, Edgerton feels that a person's subjective sense of well-being may derive more from personal attributes than environmental factors and that we need to uncouple objective standards of quality from the subjective experience of well-being.

Laird Heal and Carol Sigelman begin their chapter with a discussion of three methodological decisions that one needs to make in measuring quality of life: the general method used (objective or subjective); who the respondent will be (person, investigator, or proxy); and the type of instrument employed (survey questionnaire or observation). The authors also discuss three methodological problems that arise in interviewing persons with mental retardation: response bias, acquiescence, and level of comprehension. The authors conclude the chapter by suggesting that multiple methods (including interviews, behavior observations, and proxy respondents) are needed to adequately measure quality of life.

In Chapter 11, Sharon Borthwick-Duffy reminds us that one cannot separate evaluation and measurement of quality of life from the use of information they provide. Thus, the definition of quality of life and the methods used to assess it are likely to have a significant impact on the lives of service recipients. In our future work in the area of quality of life measurement we need to ensure that we are clear about the purposes of quality of life evaluations, are comprehensive in our assessment techniques, and factor individual and group differences into our measurement and application efforts.

As you read the following six chapters, keep in mind that measuring a multifaceted concept such as quality of life presents a number of methodological challenges. How well one measures that concept depends upon a number of factors that I've collapsed into six questions that you will want to ask yourself when reading this section on measurement.

1. What is being measured? Do the indicators being assessed flow logically from the investigator's definition, conceptualization, or model of quality of life?

2. Which assessment methods and models are used?

3. Is the person the focus of the assessment and the primary respondent?

4. Are assessment strategies used that overcome—or control for—the potential for response bias or perseveration among persons with mental retardation, as well as the receptive and expressive skill level of the respondent?

5. What measurement standards are reported for the instrument or method used? We should be especially concerned with reported reliability and validity.

6. What are the suggested uses (that is, utility) of the data? Are the data, for example, used for comparison (and if so, what is the standardization/normative group), understanding, or program improvement purposes?

Attempts to Conceptualize and Measure Quality of Life

Carolyn Hughes and Bogseon Hwang
Vanderbilt University

Recent expansion of (re)habilitation programs for persons with disabilities to include quality outcomes has brought the concept of quality of life into major disability policy and research arenas. However, the empirical and conceptual literature offers no consensus with respect to the definition or conceptual framework of the quality of life concept. As stated by Borthwick-Duffy (1989),

> ...quality of life is a subjective concept, the definition of which has been dependent on the perspectives and biases of the persons doing the evaluation. The diversity of quality of life criteria and outcome measures has been described as almost researcher specific.
>
> (p. 352)

In addition, although practitioners wish to determine program effectiveness, no consensus dimensions exist in the literature by which to measure a person's quality of life or judge the quality of the person's life (cf. Dennis, Williams, Giangreco, & Cloninger, 1993; Halpern, 1993). Researchers have argued that individuals' unique perceptions influence their conceptions of the quality of their lives, confounding the establishment of a universally-accepted conceptual model of quality of life (Sinnott-Oswald, Gliner, & Spencer, 1991). Although specific events that influence the quality of one's life may vary across individuals and their life spans (see Stark & Faulkner, this volume), we contend that agreement may be reached regarding fundamental dimensions that comprise quality of life (Hughes, Hwang, Kim, Eisenman, & Killian, 1995). Therefore, in this chapter we attempt to establish (a) a consensus list of components that comprise a model of quality of life as derived from the literature, and (b) a taxonomy of empirical measures of quality of life that have been addressed by researchers. The chapter reports briefly the review procedures, findings, and implications of our literature synthesis (see Hughes et al., 1995, for a more detailed description of procedures and a list of reviewed studies).

Review Procedures

Conceptual Model

Utilizing literature search techniques and reliability assessments recommended by Cooper (1989), we identified 44 definitions of quality of life of persons with or without disabilities in the community psychology, community integration, mental health, and employment literature from 1970 through 1993. Aggregation of the definitions resulted in 15 dimensions of quality of life (in descending frequency of support): psychological well-being and personal satisfaction; social relationships and interaction; employment; physical and material well-being; self-determination, autonomy, and personal choice; personal competence, community adjustment, and independent living skills; community integration; social acceptance, social status, and ecological fit; personal development and fulfillment; residential environment; recreation and leisure; normalization; individual and social demographic indicators; civic responsibility; and support services received.

These dimensions and their corresponding components served as the conceptual framework for the ensuing review of the literature and were proposed as a consensus list of components of quality of life as derived from a broad-based, multidisciplinary literature.

Literature Search and Analysis

In order to minimize bias in selection of studies that assessed quality of life components among persons with dis-

abilities, multiple methods (Cooper, 1989) were utilized to locate empirical studies published in refereed journals during 1970-1993, which is the period representing a significant increase in quality of life publications. The search included (a) a computer search of the Educational Resources Information Center (ERIC) and PsycLIT databases, (b) a manual review of selected journals, and (c) an ancestral search (Cooper, 1989) of reference lists from identified articles and relevant texts. The 87 articles identified through the search met five criteria (Hughes et al., 1995), and were analyzed according to participant characteristics, assessment variables, and quality of life components judged to conform to the conceptual framework. Reliability was assessed throughout each search and analysis procedure.

Findings

Participants

Of over 9,000 individuals whose quality of life was assessed across the 87 studies, only 5% were diagnosed with a disability other than mental retardation. Additionally, findings revealed that the average age of participants was 33 years, that most participants lived in supervised community-based housing (83%), and that the employment status or daytime activities of participants rarely were reported. Based upon these findings, we suggest that investigations should assess the quality of lives of persons with disabilities other than mental retardation (e.g., learning disabilities, chronic mental illness, blindness) and provide information on peoples' daily activity patterns (cf. Kennedy, Horner, & Newton, 1989).

Types of Assessments

Most investigations were survey or follow-up studies that employed either *(continued on page 57)*

(continued on page 57)

Table 6.1

Dimensions, Components, and Representative Measures
of Quality of Life

Dimension and Component	Representative Measure	Number of Different Measures	Frequency of Measures
SOCIAL RELATIONSHIPS AND INTERACTION		198 (15.9)[a]	305 (13.3)[b]
Friendship	Number of friends with and without disabilities, variety of friends, having a best friend	33	62
Interpersonal relationships	Number of relationships, having a girlfriend or boyfriend, relationships with neighbors	32	46
Social interaction	Frequency of interacting with friends, interaction with family, group size during social interaction	31	51
Interpersonal and social activities	Type of activities engaged in, eating out with family or friends, visiting with others	30	32
Social support networks	Extent of involvement of family member, sources of social support, number of people in social support network	29	43
Social skills	Getting along with others, making friends, initiating social interaction	28	50
Type of social support received	Personal and emotional support, being helped to maintain level of self-care, reliance on benefactor or advocate	11	14
Affection	Smiling when interacting, touching a person in a friendly, appropriate manner	3	3
Social responsibility	Having social responsibility	1	4
Interdependence	Not assessed	0	0
Opportunity for participation in social activities	Not assessed	0	0
PSYCHOLOGICAL WELL-BEING AND PERSONAL SATISFACTION		183 (14.7)	293 (12.8)
Life satisfaction	Satisfaction with residential situation, satisfaction with friendships, satisfaction with leisure and free time activities	88	169
Feelings	Feeling lonely, feeling depressed, feeling "on top of the world"	28	34
Perception of one's life situation	Perceived level of independence, perceived well-being, perceived level of feeling "normal"	24	30
Personal values	Perceived importance of getting recognition on the job, aspirations for independence, perceived importance of interpersonal relationships	22	25

Note. From "Quality of Life in Applied Research: Conceptual Model and Analysis of Measures" by C. Hughes, B. Hwang, J. Kim, L.T. Eisenman, and D.J. Killian, 1995, *American Journal of Mental Retardation, 99,* 623-641. Reprinted by permission.

[a] Percentage of total measures.   [b] Percentage of total frequency of measures.

Table 6.1 (continued)

Self-concept	Self-confidence, self-esteem, body image	7	16
Mental health	Emotional stability, coping with anger, verbalizing feelings	6	7
Sense of general well-being	Zest for life, enjoyment of life, qualitative dimension of life	4	7
Happiness and contentment	Maintaining personal happiness, general feeling of happiness	3	4
Personal dignity	Feeling of personal dignity	1	1
EMPLOYMENT		150 (12.1)	226 (9.9)
Job satisfaction	Satisfaction with wages, satisfaction with opportunities for promotion, responding positively toward going to work	30	54
Vocational skills	Job initiative, attendance, job skills	22	36
Support at the worksite	Social support network at work, family support at work, employer support	17	20
Social interaction at worksite	Frequency of social interaction at work, having friends at work, interacting with co-workers and supervisor during work	15	23
Employment-related interpersonal skills	Getting along with others at work, physical appearance at work, communication skills	14	17
Working environment and conditions	Wages, number of co-workers, type of supervision	13	21
Employee history and characteristics	Length of employment, employee health, promotions received	11	13
Work performance	Productivity, quality of work, consistency of work performance	9	14
Job characteristics and job requirements	Job type, task demands, worker's description of job tasks	6	9
Positive effects of job on employee	Increased self-worth of employee, improved worker attitudes, increased employee independence	5	6
Opportunity for advancement	Upward mobility, opportunity for advancement on the job	3	4
Worksite integration	Level of integration at the worksite, involvement of co-workers without disabilities	2	4
Job match	Match between worker's preference and job held	1	1
Job prestige and status	Employment status	1	1
Perceived role in work environment	Employee's perceived importance of work to employer	1	3
Job challenge	Not assessed	0	0
SELF-DETERMINATION, AUTONOMY, AND PERSONAL CHOICE		128 (10.3)	179 (7.8)
Personal control and autonomy	Having control of when to go to bed and when to get up, being able to refuse entry into one's room, being allowed to go alone to places in the community	45	65
Preference and choice	Preference for spending time alone, choosing with whom to live, choosing own menu	29	36

Independence	Level of independence when choosing home, level of independence when banking, self-sufficiency	26	45
Personal freedom	Freedom to choose to go or not to go on group outings, freedom to take risks, freedom from restrictiveness and routines	11	11
Personal decision making and problem solving	Decision-making skills, personal problem solving, deciding how to handle one's money	7	8
Self-direction	Goal setting, self-control, self-management	5	9
Opportunity for expressing preference	Opportunity to attend IPP meeting, opportunity to voice selection of television shows, opportunity to individualize routine	3	3
Opportunity to live independently	Opportunity to live alone	2	2
Empowerment	Not assessed	0	0
RECREATION AND LEISURE		100 (8.1)	264 (11.5)
Type of activity	Watching television, visiting friends, going to a movie	91	252
Opportunity for recreation and leisure	Availability of leisure activities, opportunity to participate in leisure activities, availability of a partner for leisure activities	4	4
Recreation and leisure skills	Leisure time skills, degree of supervision needed	3	6
Quality of activities	Frequency of participation, active participation versus "being kept busy"	2	2
PERSONAL COMPETENCE, COMMUNITY ADJUSTMENT, AND INDEPENDENT LIVING SKILLS		92 (7.4)	274 (12.0)
Domestic skills	Preparing meals, doing laundry, cleaning house	23	71
Self-care skills	Eating, grooming, selecting clothes	18	85
Communication and language skills	Receptive language skills, mode of communication, written language skills	13	28
Personal finance skills	Money management, having a credit card, making purchases	13	33
Independent living skills	Shopping for groceries, able to work, frequency of performing daily living skills	9	27
Survival skills	Time management, using telephone, taking safety precautions	7	12
Adaptive functioning	Ambulatory skills, continence, adaptability	4	5
Personal competence	Coping skills, managing day-to-day needs	3	4
Cognitive skills	General cognition	1	5
Responsibility	Personal responsibility	1	4
RESIDENTIAL ENVIRONMENT		92 (7.4)	149 (6.5)
Living conditions	Number of co-residents, sense of unity and cohesion in a home, living in a healthy, safe place	70	84
Residential environment	Proximity of services to residence, urban versus rural environment, physical integration of home into neighborhood setting	14	24

Table 6.1 (continued)

Living arrangement	Supervised apartment, living independently, living with parents	8	41
COMMUNITY INTEGRATION		72 (5.8)	159 (7.0)
Community integration and participation	Frequency of visiting church or synagogue, frequency of visiting friends and relatives, use of resources/facilities in the community	45	110
Mobility	Frequency of using public transportation, moving around community safely and independently, ability to leave a building independently or with assistance	12	24
Community living skills	Using telephone, frequency of performing community living skills, adapting to community life	10	23
Opportunity for participation in community activities	Isolated settings in which public interaction not possible, opportunity to engage in community	2	2
NORMALIZATION		65 (5.2)	85 (3.7)
Activity patterns	Age appropriateness of activities, routines, and rhythms; variety of activities; purpose of activities (functional, social, isolated)	42	42
Normalized life-style	Variation in times getting up and going to bed throughout the week; privacy; attending leisure activities alone, with support person, with another resident, or with all residents	17	17
Normalized service models	Staff attitudes toward activities promoting independence and normalization, use of socially appropriate terms to refer to clients, application of normalization principles by residence	6	6
SUPPORT SERVICES RECEIVED		61 (4.9)	89 (3.9)
Services received/needed	Income support (SSI) received per month, home assistance, health services received	43	69
Support staff characteristics	Staff support for facilitating positive relationships at home, staff turnover, home care providers' expectations of residents	10	12
Quality of care (services)	Respect for individual's personal dignity, residents' perception of staff support, individualization of services	8	8
INDIVIDUAL AND SOCIAL DEMOGRAPHIC INDICATORS		60 (4.8)	202 (8.8)
Individual demographics	Age, gender, income earned	34	170
Environmental demographics	Community characteristics, access to community facilities/activities, cost of public transportation	21	25
Individual characteristics	Initiative at work or home, individual's persistence, degree to which behavior problems are manageable	4	5
Family characteristics	Family income	1	2

PERSONAL DEVELOPMENT AND FULFILLMENT		15 (1.2)	24 (1.1)
Instructional opportunity	Independent living skills training, employment skills training, access to classes	5	5
Academic skills	Reading and writing skills, improving academic skills	3	10
Educational attainment	Attending school, frequency of attending educational classes, educational program enrolled in	3	5
Spiritual and personal fulfillment	Engaged in self-improvement, maintaining personal interests	2	2
Access to a stimulating environment	Degree of stimulation of community living	1	1
Opportunity for personal development and fulfillment	Freedom to try new tasks and develop new skills	1	1
Creativity	Not assessed	0	0
SOCIAL ACCEPTANCE, SOCIAL STATUS, AND ECOLOGICAL FIT		12 (1.0)	15 (.7)
Social acceptance	Social acceptance on the job, people's response to resident in public, neighbors' responding to resident in a friendly, accepting manner	8	10
Social role functions	Contributing to the community, producing work that contributes to a household or community	3	4
Respect	Mutual respect among staff and residents	1	1
Goodness of fit between person and environment	Not assessed	0	0
PHYSICAL AND MATERIAL WELL-BEING		9 (.7)	15 (.7)
Physical health	Weight, blood pressure, physical development	7	13
Personal safety	Safety from abuse, freedom from exploitation	2	2
Financial security	Not assessed	0	0
Food, clothing, and shelter	Not assessed	0	0
CIVIC RESPONSIBILITY		6 (.5)	7 (.31)
Asserting and performing civic rights and responsibilities	Rate of court appearances, history of arrests, voting	6	7
Opportunity for civic activities	Not assessed	0	0
TOTAL		1243 (100)	2286 (100)

(continued from page 52)

interviews or questionnaires; few studies used direct observation methods. Participants responded alone or with assistance in 60% of the interviews or questionnaires; parents, guardians, or informed others responded in the remaining 40%. Only 28% of studies established both reliability and validity of assessments used. These findings suggest that assessment of quality of life should involve triangulation of methods and multiple sources of information. Findings derived from interviews and questionnaires should be corroborated by direct observation, perhaps utilizing ethnographic procedures, to minimize bias and increase reliability and validity of assessments. Additional methodological concerns in assessing quality of life are addressed in Heal and Sigelman's chapter on methodological issues in this volume.

Measures of Quality of Life

Table 6.1 displays the dimensions and corresponding components of quality of life that comprise the conceptual framework used to review the studies. Representative measures of quality of life identified in the reviewed studies, the number of different measures identified for each component of quality of life, and the frequency with which each measure was measured across studies are also displayed.

Dimensions of quality of life proposed in the conceptual framework were strongly supported by the frequency with which empirical measures were taken. Correspondence typically was observed between the number of different measures assessed per dimension and the frequency with which measures were assessed. The greatest number of different measures ($N = 198$) and highest frequency of measures ($N = 305$) were associated with social relationships and interaction. In some

cases, relatively few measures were assessed with comparative frequency. For example, 92 different measures of personal incompetence, community adjustment, and independent living skills were measured a total of 274 times across studies. Interestingly, the single component of quality of life with the greatest number of different measures ($N = 91$) and most frequent measures ($N = 252$) was type of recreational and leisure activities (see recreation and leisure), followed by life satisfaction (a component of psychological well-being and personal satisfaction) (number of different measures = 88; frequency of measures = 169). A few components of the model were not assessed at all, such as interdependence, opportunity for participation in social or civic activities, empowerment, goodness of fit between person and environment, and financial security.

Implications

Conceptual Model of Quality of Life

Importantly, results of our literature review indicated that a proposed conceptual model of quality of life derived from a cross-disciplinary literature base was supported by empirical measures, resulting in a taxonomy of measures of quality of life (Table 6.1). Based upon these findings, we propose that the fundamental dimensions (outcomes) of a model of quality of life may have relevance for persons with or without disabilities, although the means for achieving these outcomes may be specific to each individual (Hughes et al., 1995). For example, our model strongly supports social relationships and interaction as a dimension of quality of life ($N = 305$ measures). Satisfaction in one's relationships (an outcome), however, may be achieved by a variety of means (processes) such as being married and frequently spending time at home with children and spouse or living alone and spending time with friends or co-workers only when at work or sporting events.

Our findings also revealed a growing consensus in the literature for a conceptual model of quality of life that is multidimensional and interactional (Chen, Bruininks, Lakin, & Hayden, 1993; McGrew, Bruininks, & Thurlow, 1992; Schalock & Genung, 1993). The broad array of measures of quality of life in Table 6.1 supports a model of quality of life that addresses the interrelationship among multiple environmental and personal factors as diverse as working in a noisy environment, having a best friend, and budgeting one's money. For example, Table 6.1 indicates that environmental factors such as working environment and conditions, living conditions, residential environment, proximity of services, and characteristics of support staff were measured frequently across reviewed studies (e.g., residential environmental factors were measured 149 times). Relatedly, personal demographic characteristics such as age, marital status, and income were measured frequently ($N = 170$), as well as personal competence, community adjustment, and independent living skills such as preparing meals, grooming, and money management. Corroborating these findings, a statistical relationship has been reported among multidimensional measures of personal competence (e.g., personal living skills, community living skills, social skills), environmental factors (e.g., support services, living arrangement, work environment), and indicators of successful community adjustment and quality of life (e.g., income, number of friends, recreation and leisure activities) among adults with mental retardation (McGrew et al., 1992). Further, the quality of one's life may be contingent on environmental factors such as standard of living or quality of available support (Goode, 1994; Schalock et al., 1994).

Purposes of a Taxonomy of Quality of Life Measures

The taxonomy of quality of life measures presented in Table 6.1 may be utilized for a variety of purposes, including program evaluation, research analysis, policy development, and meeting individualized needs.

Program evaluation. Based upon the taxonomy, a checklist could be developed to guide program development as well as to evaluate the effectiveness of services in enhancing quality of life. Further, this checklist could ensure that evaluation was relevant to individuals' lives rather than to compliance or monitoring issues (Goode, 1994). To illustrate, using the taxonomy in Table 6.1 as a guide, one may observe that a young woman living in a group home rarely participates in community activities. Further assessment may reveal that she has limited opportunity to leave home, no transportation skills, and little knowledge of community resources. The taxonomy could direct programming efforts to assess the woman's preferences for community involvement, teach her community and transportation skills, provide opportunities and necessary support to engage in community activities, and monitor and evaluate her progress and satisfaction.

Research analysis. A conceptual model of quality of life is critical to advancing our research efforts by allowing us to summarize and compare findings across studies. Borthwick-Duffy (1989) argued that studies of community integration have investigated a variety of variables including "adjustment," "adaption," "success," and "quality of life." These variables have indistinguishable operational measures (e.g., friendships);

yet without a common conceptual framework, the relationship among studies is ambiguous. The taxonomy of measures in Table 6.1 allows us to aggregate, compare, and contrast findings across studies related to quality of life.

Policy development. The taxonomy of quality of life measures could be instrumental in guiding policy by identifying unmet needs that may be used to influence resource allocation decisions. Because dimensions of quality of life may comprise the most critical issues in the disabilities field (Goode, 1994), a conceptual model of quality of life could produce powerful social policy implications, especially considering that quality of life has gained acceptance nationally and internationally as a philosophical guide and legal principle in policy formation. Further, a conceptual model of quality of life could be used to organize outcome data that could serve to protect from budget cuts services that result in enhanced quality of life.

Individual needs. A taxonomy of quality of life measures could be tailored to meet individuals' needs, environments, and preferences. For example, the residential components of the quality of life model may be more relevant than employment factors to some individuals or contexts. Additionally, the relevance of a dimension may change over time for an individual. For example, employment may become less of a focus than recreation and leisure as one becomes older. Similarly, some cultures may place more emphasis on a dimension like social interaction than on work. The model allows prioritizing and focusing upon the dimensions of quality of life that are most relevant to a particular individual within a particular context.

Recommendations for Future Efforts

If frequency of measures indicates the perceived value of a dimension of quality of life, practitioners and researchers are investing their efforts in important areas (e.g., satisfaction with work, services, and living environment; personal control and autonomy; leisure and recreational activities; see Table 6.1). However, future programming efforts need to address components of quality of life that are valued but receive limited programming focus, such as the following: (a) empowerment, (b) opportunity (e.g., to express preference, to live independently, to engage in community activities); (c) the quality associated with a dimension such as one's residential environment, social relationships, or community integration experiences; (d) personal choice; and (e) financial security.

In summary, this chapter describes an aggregation of components of quality of life into a conceptual model and taxonomy of empirical measures. The conceptual model of quality of life proposed provides an impetus for program, research, and policy activities that may profoundly affect the disability field. Ultimately, the usefulness of the taxonomy will be measured by its contribution to efforts to improve the quality of life experienced by people with disabilities.

References

Borthwick-Duffy, S.A. (1989). Quality of life: The residential environment. In W.E. Kiernan & R.L. Schalock (Eds.), *Economics, industry, and disability: A look ahead* (pp. 351-363). Baltimore: Brookes.

Chen, T.H., Bruininks, R.H., Lakin, K.C., & Hayden, M. (1993). Personal competencies and community participation in small community residential programs: A multiple discriminant analysis. *American Journal on Mental Retardation, 98,* 390-399.

Cooper, H.M. (1989). *Integrating research: A guide for literature reviews* (2nd ed.). Newbury Park, CA: Sage.

Dennis, R.E., Williams, W., Giangreco, M.F., & Cloninger, C.J. (1993). Quality of life as context for planning and evaluation of services for people with disabilities. *Exceptional Children, 59,* 499-512.

Goode, D. (1994). The national quality of life for persons with disabilities project: A quality of life agenda for the United States. In D. Goode (Ed.), *Quality of life for persons with disabilities: International perspectives and issues* (pp. 139-161). Cambridge, MA: Brookline Books.

Halpern, A.S. (1993). Quality of life as a conceptual framework for evaluating transition outcomes. *Exceptional Children, 59,* 486-498.

Hughes, C., Hwang, B., Kim, J., Eisenman, L.T., & Killian, D.J. (1995). Quality of life in applied research: A review and analysis of empirical measures. *American Journal on Mental Retardation, 99,* 623-641.

Kennedy, C.H., Horner, R.H., & Newton, J.S. (1989). Social contacts of adults with severe disabilities living in the community: A descriptive analysis of relationship patterns. *Journal of the Association for Persons with Severe Handicaps, 14,* 190-196.

McGrew, K.S., Bruininks, R.H., & Thurlow, M.L. (1992). Relationship between measures of adaptive functioning and community adjustment for adults with mental retardation. *Exceptional Children, 58,* 517-529.

Schalock, R.L., & Genung, L.T. (1993). Placement from a community-based mental retardation program: A 15-year follow-up. *American Journal on Mental Retardation, 98,* 400-407.

Schalock, R.L., Stark, J.A., Snell, M.E., Coulter, D.L., Polloway, E.A., Luckasson, R., Reiss, S., & Spitalnik, D.M. (1994). The changing conception of mental retardation: Implications for the field. *Mental Retardation, 32,* 181-193.

Sinnott-Oswald, M., Gliner, J.A., & Spencer, K.C. (1991). Supported and sheltered employment: Quality of life issues among workers with disabilities. *Education and Training in Mental Retardation, 26,* 388-397.

Assessment of Quality of Life

David Felce and Jonathan Perry
Welsh Centre for Learning Disabilities Applied Research Unit
University of Wales College of Medicine

Quality of life has emerged as a potentially unifying concept in assessing the impact of care processes on the character of people's day-to-day lives. Although the way it is defined varies, it can serve to bring together developmental change in individuals with a disability and their identities; in the nature of their circumstances, experience, and life-style; and in their perceptions about themselves, their circumstances, experiences, and life-styles.

However, quality of life is still an imprecise concept. Whether it refers to the life conditions and life-style of an individual or to that person's subjective appraisal of their conditions and way of life is an open question acknowledged by Landesman's (1986) call for a concerted effort to explore the meaning of the two concepts (quality of life and life satisfaction). Moreover, the scope for divergence increases in the attempt to render quality of life measurable. In reviewing the status of the methodology prior to their own scale development, Cummins, McCabe, Romeo, and Gullone (1994) commented on the variation in use of the term within and across the psychological, sociological, and medical literature.

We have no wish to add to the number of possible formulations. Indeed, the content of our chapter comes out of an attempt at synthesis; a desire to take account of the considerable writing on this topic in recent years not only in the mental retardation literature (e.g., Borthwick-Duffy, 1992; Brown, 1988; Brown, Bayer, & MacFarlane, 1989; Goode, 1988, 1994; Schalock, 1990), but also in that concerned with other defined groups (e.g., Bigelow, McFarland, & Olson, 1991; Parmenter, 1988) and with society as a whole (e.g., Campbell, Converse, & Rodgers, 1976). We have drawn selectively on this literature to identify definitional themes and to construct a model of quality of life based on common ground (Felce & Perry, 1995). Our formulation comprises a three element model in which personal values, life conditions, and personal satisfaction interact to determine quality of life.

Quality of Life: Objective Conditions, Subjective Appraisal, and Personal Values

There is broad agreement that quality of life is a multidimensional construct. We have found it useful to consider three major dimensions to provide a framework for thinking about quality of life and its assessment:

1. *Objective life conditions* is the objective description of individuals and their circumstances.

2. *Subjective well-being is* personal satisfaction with such life conditions or lifestyle.

3. *Personal values and aspirations* is the relative importance to an individual of objective life conditions and subjective well-being with regard to a given aspect of life.

This three-component model, summarized in Figure 7.1, builds on other formulations summarized by Borthwick-Duffy (1992). The first component suggests that quality of life is the sum of the objectively measurable life conditions experienced by an individual. Subjective response to such conditions is the domain of personal satisfaction with life. This model is compatible with the argument that no citizen can be guaranteed satisfaction with life but only the right to life and reasonable life conditions. Life conditions may well affect personal satisfac-

tion, but neither this potential relationship nor the subjective appraisal itself is germane to quality of life assessment. General indicators of quality of life may, therefore, be established by the assessment of a variety of life conditions across the population. The life conditions of a particular individual or subgroup would be located by comparing their position to the total population distribution.

Figure 7.1
A Model of Quality of Life

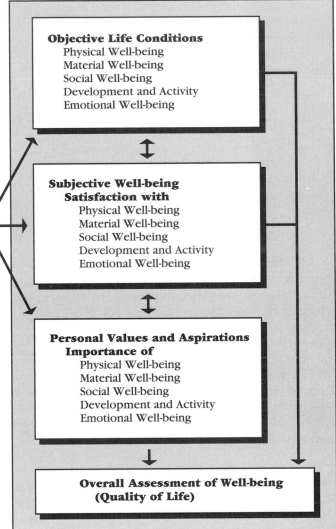

However, many authors caution against assuming that there are objective standards by which one can define a decent or reasonable quality of life (see, for example, Edgerton, 1990). Because individuals differ in what they find important, satisfaction with life, as reflected in the second component, is an essential criterion of quality of life. Overall satisfaction with life may reflect satisfaction in a number of life domains. Such a conceptualization has been used in work on the well-being of the general population. Flanagan (1978) considered satisfaction with material comforts, health, work, recreation, learning, and creative expression. Campbell (1981) included a similar but more extensive coverage of domain areas: marriage, family life, friendships, standard of living, work, neighborhood, city or town of residence, the state of the nation, housing, education, health, and the self. It may be hypothesized that satisfaction is influenced by external and objectively quantifiable life conditions, and such a model has been tested (Allen, Bentler, & Gutek, 1985).

Yet, treating expressed satisfaction as a commentary on the acceptability of life conditions experienced is not unproblematic. First, reports of well-being may owe more to internal temperament than to external conditions. In commenting on the possible independence between life conditions and subjective reports of well-being, Edgerton (1990) cites his and others' research (Costa, McCrae, & Zonderman, 1987; Keogh & Pullis, 1980; Lazarus & Lannier, 1979) to sustain the argument that significant changes in life conditions may only induce temporary changes in reports of well-being. Regression to a characteristic level will occur in time and, hence, the longitudinal pattern is relatively stable with the best predictor of current satisfaction being its past rating. Far from being the subtle indicator of quality of life that it is often

assumed to be, satisfaction may be an unresponsive indicator, sensitive only to gross and immediate changes in life conditions.

Second, satisfaction is a measure of comparison, over time and across demographic boundaries. Even when expressions of satisfaction may relate to external conditions rather than temperament, it is impossible to divorce them from their context. In other words, they reflect a frame of reference, which is itself shaped by experience. One, therefore, cannot assume that a person's frame of reference will embrace all possibilities; it is affected by the judgment of what is possible and typical for a person in that situation. Experience may teach that change is possible, and low satisfaction in this case may indicate that the desired change has not been achieved, while high satisfaction may indicate that it has. In a simple illustration, a person may be satisfied with his or her wages until he or she discovers that a colleague of equivalent seniority, competence, and responsibilities at work earns significantly more. The shift in satisfaction results from a previously stable comparison with a defined reference group or peer group being overturned. The feeling of dissatisfaction may continue until the now possible prospect of increased remuneration is achieved. However, experience may also teach that change is not possible; that there are pervasive life conditions that are typical for the individual and his or her class or peer group. Under such circumstances, expressions of satisfaction may adjust to habitual life conditions even if those conditions are towards the least-favored end of the distribution for the population as a whole. Quality of life defined as synonymous with personal satisfaction, without regard to widely different life conditions, is a less appealing formulation if account is not taken of the distribution of such life conditions across sections of the population and of the relative permanence of such distributions throughout the lives of individuals and across generations.

Stated otherwise, the ability to change life conditions independently in line according to personal preference, upon which the primacy of subjective appraisal as the best quality of life indicator rests, cannot be assumed. Many societal groups are disadvantaged economically, educationally, or by class, racial origin, or other factors. For such groups, the autonomy to maintain or change life conditions in line with subjective appraisal is frequently constrained. Most people with substantial disabilities lack independence and experience constrained opportunities and reduced autonomy, a combination that frequently results in their being forced to inhabit worlds of other people's construction. Certainly, at this extreme, one cannot conclude that lifestyle necessarily reflects personal choice.

This logic leads to the prediction that socially devalued people, whose circumstances, status, and options may make them particularly prone to having low expectations, would report satisfaction rather than dissatisfaction even under adverse life conditions. Research on adults with moderate or mild mental retardation living relatively independently has provided a picture consistent with this prediction (Schalock & Keith, 1993). Studies that have explored the views of people with developmental disabilities have shown that individuals remain philosophical or satisfied about the present and remarkably optimistic about the future despite the adverse conditions in which they live, including poverty, poor housing, threats to health and safety, victimization, social isolation, personal loss, and failure to gain or retain employment (Close & Halpern, 1988; Edgerton, Bollinger, & Herr, 1984; Flynn,

1989). Holland (1990) found that residents of a range of living environments, that differed markedly on many objective characteristics from impoverished traditional hospital wards to typical community housing, expressed equally high satisfaction with their circumstances. A definition of quality of life which ignores objective assessment of life conditions may, therefore, not provide the level of safeguard for vulnerable people that should be associated with a measure that is to be accepted as the criterion for the adequacy of social policy in general and the design and level of service support in particular.

Nevertheless, personal appraisal has a validity for which there is no substitute if one person's values are not to be imposed on another. In view of the weaknesses in defining quality of life in terms of either life conditions or satisfaction, it may be best seen as a combination of objective and subjective components. Such a formulation is commonly found (e.g., Bigelow et al., 1991; Schalock, 1994; Schalock & Keith, 1993). The Quality of Life Questionnaire (Schalock & Keith, 1993) has four sections, three of which focus on objective data concerned with independence/decision-making, productivity, and community integration. The fourth section addresses satisfaction rated on a three-point scale in 10 areas: an overall view on life, how much enjoyment respondents derive from it, how well off they are compared to others, whether most events or activities are rewarding or not, their satisfaction with their living arrangements, how well they are treated by neighbors, whether their education prepared them for what they are currently doing, the extent of their problems, whether they feel lonely, and whether they feel out of place in social situations.

However, how to combine objective or subjective appraisals across issues of relevance is not specified in our model's first two components. Measures that lack a basis for ranking the importance that different individuals give to various aspects of their overall situation are frequently given equal weighting, as in the Schalock and Keith (1993) scale described above. Alternatively, assumptions about the relative importance of different concerns may be used to generate a weighting structure. In both cases, the method of combining items in the overall assessment can be criticized as somewhat arbitrary. As a consequence, Cummins (1993) has suggested that the conceptualization of quality of life should comprise objective and subjective assessment as well as the relative importance the individual places on the various objective and subjective aspects considered across life domains.

This differential weighting approach is consistent with the concept that well-being stems from the degree of fit between individuals' perceptions of their objective situations and their needs, aspirations, or values (Andrews & Withey, 1976; Campbell et al., 1976). Moreover, the principle of taking account of an individual's scale of values is relevant to both the objective and subjective facets of assessment; the relative weight given to objective and subjective aspects of the same issue need not be similar. For example, someone with nonmaterial values may give a low weight to size of income but a high weight to satisfaction with income (on the basis of the importance of income being sufficient to meet needs). Conversely, a person who considers money to be important may give a high weight to size of income but a low weight to satisfaction with income (he or she may be accustomed to never being satisfied with his or her income). Thus, the model's third component broadens the application of the goodness-of-fit approach by using individual value struc-

tures and aspirations to weight the importance of both objective and subjective components. In so doing, the concern that only individuals can decide the trade-off between competing aspects of their own personal welfare is met.

The Complexity of Life Reflected in an Analysis of Life Domains

Although authors may vary on how they have conceptualized quality of life, there is a considerable overlap among them on how relevant life domains may be categorized and enumerated. Based on a recent review of the literature (Felce & Perry, 1995) a five-way categorization of life domains is relevant to developing a conceptual model of quality of life:

1. *Physical well-being*, which subsumes health, fitness, mobility, and personal safety. Fitness and mobility both relate to aspects of physical ability and may be best defined as functional capacities relative to specific activities. These aspects may, therefore, partially overlap with the consideration of development and activity below. Physical safety is the degree of freedom from injury or harm; its assessment may overlap with the assessment of neighborhood context considered in the next domain area.

2. *Material well-being*, which subsumes finance and income, various aspects of the quality of the living environment, transport, and security and tenure, all issues of importance to most members of the population. Housing quality, the level of furnishings, equipment, and possessions, and the character of the neighborhood are all relevant aspects of environmental quality.

3. *Social well-being,* which includes two major dimensions: (a) the quality and breadth of interpersonal relationships—within household life, with family and relatives, and with friends and acquaintances; and (b) community involvement— community activities undertaken and the level of acceptance or support given by the community.

4. *Development and activity,* which is concerned with the acquisition and use of skills. Competence or the development of adaptive behavior is linked to self-determination (independence and the concomitant abilities to exercise choice or control), productivity, and contribution. All may be expressed through the pursuit of functional activities in different arenas such as home, work, leisure, and education.

5. *Emotional well-being*, which subsumes affect, fulfillment, stress and mental state, self-esteem, status and respect, religious faith, and sexuality. Fulfillment may overlap with achievement of social and functional pursuits. Degree of stress, which in this version replaces satisfaction included in our earlier framework, reflects the conditions under which social and functional activities are pursued. Satisfaction is used throughout this chapter as a major dimension to include subjective appraisal across the content areas of all five domains. It is, therefore, redundant as an item to be considered within the categorization of life domains. However, stress may affect the degree to which one derives satisfaction from life and may contribute to or detract from emotional well-being.

Quality of Life: A Multidimensional, Multielement Framework

The model in Figure 7.1 incorporates the five categories of life-style elements considered in the three dimensions of quality of life discussed. Quality of life is defined as an overall general well-being that comprises objective descriptors and subjective evaluations of physical, material, social, and emotional well-being together with the extent of development and activity, all weighted by a personal set of values. As shown in Figure 7.1, *these dimensions are shown in dynamic interaction with each other and as potentially interdependent at all times*. A change in one dimension may affect a person's position on another. For example, a change in some objective facet of life such as increasing material well-being may promote a person's sense of satisfaction. Similarly, it may lead to a complementary change in the person's scale of values. Alternatively, increasing material well-being associated with a deteriorating sense of satisfaction may prompt a change in values in the opposite direction. Changes in values may initiate changes in satisfaction and precipitate changes in objective circumstance. For example, a person may come to believe in a nonmaterialist way of life as a better mode of existence, become less satisfied with his or her range of functional pursuits, change his or her job, and lower his or her material standards.

As well as affecting each other, each dimension is capable of being influenced by a range of external factors that define the individual's biological make-up, developmental and cultural history, and current environment. Such external influences might include genetic, social, and material inheritance, age and maturation, development, employment, peer influences and reference points, and other social, economic, and political variables. As the three elements that define quality of life are all open to external influence, assessment of all three is necessary to any measurement system purporting to examine or rate quality of life. Knowledge of one set cannot predict another, and the relationships between them may not remain constant over time.

Application of Quality of Life Measurement

Some commentators within the mental retardation field have doubted the usefulness of the quality of life concept. Wolfensberger (1994), for example, has warned that the use of the term has become so charged that rational debate is becoming inhibited, that contaminating associations are becoming too numerous, and that the notions of quality of life and value of life are being dangerously confused to justify withdrawal of effort and resources, or even life itself, from those who cannot attain certain life-style characteristics. Wolfensberger also draws attention to the origins of the quality of life concept in the concern to encapsulate the well-being of populations rather than individuals. The later shift towards an individual focus has brought attendant concerns that quality of life, once operationalized, will be imposed without regard to individual difference. This concern may well affect how commentators define the concept and make them unwilling to include any perspective other than individual subjective appraisal. In part, this reflects the position adopted by Taylor (1994), who has argued in favor of quality of life as a sensitizing concept but against its formulation in measurable terms on the grounds that its operationalization will

inevitably diminish its conceptual scope and reduce it to a reification.

It is important, therefore, to ensure that conceptual clarity is attained, free from distortion resulting from concerns about possible misuses of the measure. How the measure is to be applied, however, should be defined in its own right. Judging quality of life is a separate issue to its measurement and calls for an explicit basis upon which the judgment is made. There is an obvious objection to an externally imposed quality of life framework replacing personal autonomy as a mechanism for making choices and determining personal circumstances. An indication that a person's quality of life is low may signal a review of the person's circumstances, but this will best be done within a process, such as personal futures planning, which supports self-determination to the maximum extent. Moreover, life conditions and satisfaction with life will inevitably vary, and neither ideal conditions nor perfect satisfaction can be arranged for or achieved by every member of a society or societal subgroup. At the individual level, therefore, quality of life may remain primarily a sensitizing concept, as Taylor (1994) has advocated. Its measurement may provide valuable data to inform the arrangements which are agreed by the person in his or her interests, but the precise arrangements made remain a matter of negotiation between vested parties.

At the aggregate level, quality of life data may have greater uses. Much service evaluation implicitly follows a utilitarian criterion of the greatest good for the greatest number. Quality of life data applied to the question of evaluating major service provision movements, such as deinstitutionalization or mainstreaming, may provide a better rubric than measures of more limited scope. Similarly, quality of life data for a defined group of interest may be compared to those for the total population to establish whether aspects of quality of life are similarly distributed or narrowly clustered either in their favor or to their disadvantage. In other words, cultural norms and ranges may provide a standard of reference. A view that an acceptable quality of life had been achieved could require that both expressed satisfaction with various aspects of life and objective descriptors of those aspects were in keeping with, or at least not inferior to, the typical for the society as a whole.

As a consequence, any conceptualization of quality of life must not be limited to a particular vulnerable or devalued societal subgroup, but should be generally applicable to the population as a whole. The task of establishing the social validity of the proposed construct will, therefore, be achieved by reference to a cross section of society rather than to any specific voice or set of interests. The five domains suggested as content categories relevant to quality of life are of a general nature and, indeed, reflect the scope of quality of life assessment as applied to the general population. This is clearly desirable from the perspective of developing a quality of life measurement system that has broad utility. The adequacy of the scope of the items needs to be examined by research which establishes indicators of quality of life that are sufficient to reflect the range of public concerns. Once achieved, such a quality of life framework would allow the comparison of the quality of life of people with disabilities to that of other citizens.

Conclusion

A model of quality of life is proposed that integrates objective and subjective indicators, collectively reflecting a broad range of life domains, through an individual ranking of the relative importance of each domain. This model accommodates concerns that objective data should not be interpreted without reference to individual difference and that expressions of satisfaction are themselves relative to the individual's temperament and the circumstances and experiences that have shaped the individual's frame of reference. Considerable agreement among writers on this topic lends confidence to the extent to which life domains relevant to the conceptualization of quality of life can be identified.

The development of a common approach to quality of life applicable across societal groups and to the total population is vital if information regarding any section of society is to be interpreted with confidence. Problems in inferring what alternative quality of life might be reasonable in the individual case are compounded by the fact that life conditions and satisfaction with life inevitably vary across individuals in all groups within society. However, aggregate data for a defined group of interest, compared to the statistical distribution for the population as a whole, can be used to reflect whether life conditions and satisfaction in various domains are typical of the general pattern or have a significantly different profile. Social policy may then respond to conspicuous inequality.

References

Allen, H.M., Bentler, P.M., & Gutek, B.A. (1985). Probing theories of individual well-being: A comparison of quality-of-life models assessing neighbourhood satisfaction. *Basic and Applied Social Psychology, 6,* 181-203.

Andrews, F.M., & Withey, S.B. (1976). *Social indicators of well-being: Americans' perceptions of life quality.* New York: Plenum.

Bigelow, D.A., McFarland, B.H., & Olson, M.M. (1991). Quality of life of community mental health program clients: Validating a measure. *Community Mental Health Journal, 27,* 43-55.

Borthwick-Duffy, S.A. (1992). Quality of life and quality of care in mental retardation. In L. Rowitz (Ed.), *Mental retardation in the year 2000* (pp. 52-65). New York: Springer-Verlag.

Brown, R.I. (1988). *Quality of life for handicapped people.* London: Croom Helm.

Brown, R.I., Bayer, M.B., & MacFarlane, C.M. (1989). *Rehabilitation programmes: The performance and quality of life of adults with developmental handicaps.* Toronto: Lugus Productions Ltd.

Campbell, A. (1981). *The sense of well-being in America.* New York: McGraw Hill.

Campbell, A., Converse, P.E., & Rodgers, W.L. (1976). *The quality of American life: Perceptions, evaluation and satisfactions.* New York: Russell Sage Foundation.

Close, D.W., & Halpern, A.S. (1988). Transitions to supported living. In M.P. Janicki, M.W. Krauss, & M.M. Seltzer (Eds.), *Community residences for persons with developmental disabilities: Here to stay* (pp. 159-172). Baltimore: Brookes.

Costa, P.T., Jr., McCrae, R.R., & Zonderman, A.B. (1987). Environmental and dispositional influences on well-being: Longitudinal follow-up of an American national sample. *British Journal of Psychology, 78,* 299-306.

Cummins, R.A. (1993). *Comprehensive quality of life scale—intellectual disability (4th ed.).* Melbourne: Psychology Research Centre.

Cummins, R.A., McCabe, M.P., Romeo, Y., & Gullone, E. (1994). The comprehensive quality of life scale (ComQol): Instrument development and psychometric evaluation on college staff and students. *Educational and Psychological Measurement, 54,* 372-382.

Edgerton, R.B. (1990). Quality of life from a longitudinal research perspective. In R.L. Schalock (Ed.), *Quality of life: Perspectives and issues* (pp. 149-160). Washington, DC: American Association on Mental Retardation.

Edgerton, R.B., Bollinger, M., & Herr, B. (1984). The cloak of competence: After two decades. *American Journal on Mental Deficiency, 88,* 345-351.

Felce, D., & Perry, J. (1995). Quality of life: Its definition and measurement. *Research in Developmental Disabilities, 16,* 51-74.

Flanagan, J.C. (1978). A research approach to improving our quality of life. *American Psychologist, 33,* 138-147.

Flynn, M. (1989). *Independent living for adults with a mental handicap: A place of my own.* London: Cassel.

Goode, D. (1988). *Quality of life: A review and synthesis of the literature.* Valhalla, NY: The Mental Retardation Institute.

Goode, D. (1994). Quality of life policy: Some issues and implications of a generic social policy concept for people with developmental disabilities. *European Journal on Mental Disability, 1,* 38-45.

Holland, A. (1990). *People with mental retardation living in community homes: Their views and the quality of the service.* Unpublished doctoral thesis, University of Loughborough.

Keogh, B.K., & Pullis, M.E. (1980). Temperament influences on the development of exceptional children. In B.K. Keogh (Ed.), *Advances in Special Education (Vol. 1)* (pp. 110-121). Greenwich, CT: JAI.

Landesman, S. (1986). Quality of life and personal life satisfaction: Definition and measurement issues. *Mental Retardation, 24,* 141-143.

Lazarus, R., & Lannier, R. (1979). Stress related transactions between person and environment. In L. Pervin & M. Lewis (Eds.), *Perspectives in international psychology* (pp. 312-329). New York: Plenum.

Parmenter, T.R. (1988). An analysis of the dimensions of quality of life for people with physical disabilities. In R.I. Brown (Ed.), *Quality of life for handicapped people* (pp. 48-61). London: Croom Helm.

Schalock, R.L. (Ed.) (1990). *Quality of life: Perspectives and issues.* Washington, DC: American Association on Mental Retardation.

Schalock, R.L. (1994). The concept of quality of life and its current applications in the field of mental retardation/developmental disabilities. In D. Goode (Ed.), *Quality of life for persons with disabilities: International perspectives and issues* (pp. 266-284). Cambridge, MA: Brookline.

Schalock, R.L., & Keith, K.D. (1993). *The Quality of Life Questionnaire.* Worthington, Ohio: IDS Publishing Co.

Taylor, S.J. (1994). In support of research on quality of life, but against QOL. In D. Goode (Ed.), *Quality of life for persons with disabilities: International perspectives and issues* (pp. 260-265). Cambridge, MA: Brookline.

Wolfensberger, W. (1994). Let's hang up "quality of life" as a hopeless term. In D. Goode (Ed.), *Quality of life for persons with disabilities: International perspectives and issues* (pp. 285-321). Cambridge, MA: Brookline.

CHAPTER 8

Measuring Quality of Life Across Cultures: Issues and Challenges

Kenneth D. Keith

Nebraska Wesleyan University

Current work in the field, including the contents of this volume, makes clear the difficulty inherent in measuring quality of life in a meaningful way—a difficulty magnified by the lack of general agreement on definitions and conceptual frameworks, even among writers within similar cultures. The challenge becomes even greater when we recognize that the concept of quality of life as a research interest exists in a psychological environment that is increasingly cross-cultural (Heal, Schalock, & Keith, 1992; Keith, Yamamoto, Okita, & Schalock, 1995). We live in a time that encourages, perhaps even demands, cross-cultural comparisons within the field of developmental disabilities (Davies, 1986; Schalock, Bartnik, Wu, Konig, Lee, & Reiter, 1990) and with other populations (Keith et al., 1995; Wolff, Rutten, & Bayers, 1992).

Although cross-cultural psychological research, including quality of life research, raises a variety of fascinating questions, it also presents some signifi-

cant challenges. Among these are the universality of findings, the equivalence of concepts, the rules and values of cultures, and the pitfall of superficiality (Lonner & Malpass, 1994). While recognizing these dangers, we must accept that the reality of increasing cultural exchange makes greater cross-cultural understanding essential (Brislin, 1993). Thus, the role of culture as a determinant of views on quality of life becomes a central issue in our efforts to study the concept across international boundaries.

The Impact of Culture

It seems well established that although objective measures of life conditions are in some respects important, they do not fully account for the individual experience of quality of life. Subjective assessment of an individual's perceptions of life experiences, including factors like relationships, community activities, physical and material well-being, and personal development (Flanagan, 1978, 1982), as well as subjective views of satisfaction and happiness (Abbey & Andrews, 1986; Myers, 1992), must also be considered. Such subjective reactions include both emotional and cognitive components—dimensions of experience that are intimately linked to cultural experience (Markus & Kitayama, 1991). For example, Triandis (1994) has noted that, "people cut the pie of experience differently if they grow in a collectivist rather than an individualistic culture" (p. 171). Experience in differing types of cultures is reflected both in the perceptions of the individual (including those with disabilities) by others in the culture (Schalock et al., 1990) and in the individual's sense of self (Triandis, 1994).

Perceptions of Others

It has been shown that in cultures viewing individuals as independent (for example, the United States and other Western cultures), people are often described in terms of traits that are relatively context-free (Markus & Kitayama, 1991). Thus, rather than describing the situation or the relational contingencies producing an individual's actions, we might simply label the person, attributing the behavior to personal characteristics. We can readily see this tendency in relation to persons with developmental disabilities—persons who are often described in our culture as simply "retarded," without reference to specific aspects of their behavior in particular contexts.

In contrast to the situation in so-called independent or individualistic cultures, people in collective or interdependent cultures (for example, a number of Asian cultures) are more likely to view individuals in terms of their behavior in specific situations or relationships (Markus & Kitayama, 1991). For example, at a time when work like that of Goddard (1912) was stigmatizing individuals with mental retardation in

Western cultures, official Japanese reports (as cited in Senoo, 1985) were stressing the importance of strong ties to relatives in provision of care for such persons.

In the interdependent culture, group membership is fundamentally significant, one's satisfaction depends heavily upon acceptance by the "in group," and members of the in group will sacrifice greatly for one of their own. In the independent culture, the person may know a wide circle of people, but not have close relationships with any of them. At the same time, no culture fails totally to acknowledge both individual and group goals (Brislin, 1993), and each cultural view has its strengths and its weaknesses (Triandis, 1994). The important point for the present discussion is the recognition that the cultural perspective provides a powerful backdrop against which a society views the individual, influencing what is seen as "good" for the individual (and the group) and how the individual is likely to be treated.

Similarly, the nature or condition of the individual may be viewed in quite different ways by various cultures. Beirne-Smith, Patton, and Ittenbach (1994), for example, cited a case reported by Keck of a non-Western perception of disability in Papua, New Guinea, where meningitis-related brain damage (Western interpretation) was seen as the result of the child's "free soul" having been frightened from the body. These two viewpoints result, of course, in disparate notions regarding treatment and perception of the person.

Sense of Self

When individuals in various cultures are asked to complete sentences starting with "I am," those in collective (interdependent) societies are likely to complete the statement with a reference to a group or a relationship ("I am a daughter," "I am a Catholic," etc.). In contrast, those in individualistic (independent) societies are likely to define themselves in terms of personal characteristics or traits ("I am kind," "I am tall," etc.) (Triandis, 1994).

Individuals seem clearly to be socialized in these differing ways in the different kinds of cultures. Parents in individualistic cultures raise their children to be independent, capable at an early age of making their own decisions, choosing their own friends, etc. In contrast, in more communal societies children are taught interdependence and reliance upon the family and other groups (Myers, 1992).

The result of these differing approaches to enculturation of children can be striking differences in the perception of self in relation to the society. Interdependent cultures may foster an emphasis on collective welfare, proper relations with others, and the needs of others, as opposed to the importance of the distinct self, separateness, and autonomy often engendered by independent cultures (Markus & Kitayama, 1991).

Taken together, these differences in group views of the individual and of the individual's sense of self may produce discrepant notions of happiness, satisfaction, or well-being—of quality of life—across cultures. This discrepancy was illustrated by Kitayama, Markus, Kurokawa, and Negishi (as cited in Matsumoto, 1994) in research examining the relationship between positive emotional feelings (happiness) and "engaged" feelings (for example, friendly or respectful feelings toward others) or "disengaged" feelings (for example, pride, superiority) in American and Japanese subjects. Among the Japanese, happiness was strongly associated with the "engaged" emotions; among Americans,

it was highly correlated with the "disengaged" emotions. These findings suggest that it would be a critical mistake to believe that the two groups are made happy by identical experiences. Special attention must therefore be given to the problems involved in measuring (or comparing) the concept of quality of life across cultures.

Measurement Problems

Schalock et al. (1990) suggested that quality of life might serve as a foundation for public policy and program practices, as well as for cross-cultural research. These assertions seem, on their surface, to be reasonable enough, but they pose some significant challenges: Can cross-cultural public policies and program practices be based on the same assumptions about quality of life? Should cross-cultural research focus on comparative data? Can similar measurement tools be employed in differing cultures?

Cultural Assumptions

Researchers in cross-cultural psychology have recognized that certain principles or truths (*etics*) are universal, and seem to be consistent across cultures; others (*emics*) are culture-bound and thus differ across cultures (Matsumoto, 1994). For example, the importance of teaching school children independent thinking might be an American emic (Brislin, 1993), but my wife, in her initial experience in teaching English to Japanese junior college students, was surprised when they consulted colleagues before answering questions in class—illustrating a group-oriented Japanese emic.

Even in the most broad and familiar of psychological constructs, cultural assumptions play an important role. For example, there are certain etic aspects associated with the concept of "intelligence" (for example, ability to solve problems), but it also has emic characteristics (for example, culturally differing emphases on speed of problem solving) that would invalidate sweeping cross-cultural generalizations (Brislin, 1993). Likewise, the role of values, certainly an important underpinning for cultural views of quality of life, may vary significantly from culture to culture (Feather, 1994). Thus, while we might agree wholeheartedly with the suggestion of Schalock et al. (1990) that personal satisfaction of persons with disabilities will be enhanced if we "stress and allow for valued social roles and activities" (p. 21), it will remain for the specific culture to inform us as to which roles and activities will be valued.

Two examples from our work will serve to illustrate the importance of cultural assumptions. First, it seems likely that the concept of loneliness may be interpreted and experienced quite differently among some independent and interdependent cultures. Children may be raised with differing types of social networks (Tietjen, 1994), and some observers expect loneliness and depression to be products of individualistic culture (cf. Myers, 1992). On the Quality of Life Questionnaire (Schalock & Keith, 1993), we ask respondents to report the frequency with which they feel lonely, and we assign lower scores to greater reported frequencies of loneliness—reflecting a prevailing American value that loneliness is a bad thing. Generalization of this value to other cultures is of course questionable, and even within American culture we must use care in interpreting the nature and complexity of loneliness (Potthoff, 1981).

Second, we have assigned higher quality of life scores to individuals who belong to more clubs and organizations, again reflecting an American community value. But, as we have noted elsewhere (Keith et al., 1995), in Japanese culture it

would perhaps be more appropriate to give a high score to an individual who is strongly loyal to a single club or organization, making the underlying cultural assumptions central to interpretation of a particular experience. We may see therefore, that just as cultural differences must be taken into account in other types of assessment among individuals with mental retardation (Beirne-Smith et al., 1994), they must also be considered in evaluating quality of life.

Comparative Data

Wolff et al. (1992), in evaluating the liveability of 22 of the world's industrial nations, asserted that their ratings were "made up of just the facts" (p. 5), and they proceeded to review an astonishing array of comparative data. However, as I have suggested earlier, and as Campbell and Kahn (1976) stated, "...it is the experience of life which gives it its quality" (p. 163). We must not be too quick to compare lest we find ourselves comparing apples and oranges.

In working with a team of translators preparing Japanese versions of our quality of life questionnaires (Keith & Schalock, 1995; Schalock & Keith, 1993), we learned that the literal translation of words is often not the same as communication of the true meaning of a word or phrase. The team often agonized over the possible ways that a particular conceptual connotation might be achieved in the second language, even when the literal translation of the language was fairly straightforward. The danger here lies not only in the possibility that one language may not have adequate terms to capture a concept from the other, but also in the possibility that the original might contain emic characteristics not readily accessible to the second culture (Brislin, 1993). If a translation does not "mean" the same thing as the original, then of course any effort to compare data from the two versions is meaningless.

In one instance (Keith et al., 1995) we dealt with the translation/meaning problem in the following way:

1. Two native Japanese graduate students in social welfare and a native Japanese professor of psychology, all bilingual, translated the Quality of Student Life Questionnaire (QSLQ) from English to Japanese, discussing and editing the items until consensus was reached on the Japanese version.

2. An independent bilingual native speaker of Japanese translated the Japanese version back to English.

3. The original QSLQ and the back-translated version were then administered to a group of native English-speaking students ($N = 26$) in a 14-day test-retest format. Half of the group completed the original QSLQ first, and half the back-translation. After 14 days, each then completed the alternate version. The Pearson product-moment correlation for the two forms administered in this way was .89 for the total scores.

A procedure of this type is intended, of course, to produce opportunity to examine the extent to which concepts "come through" in the translation (Brislin, 1993), and can lend some credence to the assumption that both groups are talking about the same thing. But the establishment of somewhat comparable meanings in data-gathering instruments still may not ensure the existence of comparable data.

Even when responding similarly to the same or comparable questions regarding their situations or perceptions, individuals across cultures may produce different answers. This apparent contradiction is related to the previously noted issue of perception of self. Across many cultures, self-serving biases are present in studies requiring self-ratings. Thus, as Myers (1992) reported, 86 percent of Australians rate themselves above average (and 1 percent below average) in job performance, 90 percent of college professors and business managers rate their own performance as superior, and most American high school students consider themselves to be among the top 10 percent in ability to get along with others.

According to Myers, similar biases have been found around the world: in France, Holland, Australia, Japan, India, China, and the United States, among others. Unfortunately, for those who might like to compare data across cultures, these biases in self-perception are not of the same magnitude across cultures—and yet, as I have suggested, it is such perceptions upon which views of quality of life are based. Thus, on questions that require comparison of oneself to others (for example, "Do you have more or fewer problems than most people?" "How successful do you think you are, compared to others?"), cultural comparisons may depend as much upon differential self- rating styles as true differences in life circumstance (Schalock & Keith, 1993). Americans may rate themselves as much as 20 percent higher than Japanese on such dimensions (Markus & Kitayama, 1991), thus complicating cross-cultural comparisons (Keith et al., 1995) and suggesting the need for careful calibration of data collection instruments and techniques.

Cross-Cultural Tools

Do the problems addressed above suggest that quality of life measurement tools have no cross-cultural generality, or that the issue of quality of life assessment across cultures is an impossible task? Possibly not. These problems do suggest, however, some compelling cautions. As

Matsumoto (1994) made clear, the ethno-centrism pervading much of our knowl-edge in American psychology has kept us from seeing alternative interpretations that arise from differing cultural contexts. If we rush to apply American standards and values to data collected using Ameri-can instruments, we are virtually certain to fail in any meaningful understanding of cross-cultural quality of life.

On the other hand, if we take ac-count of cultural context and differential views of self, and if we use data not for mere quantitative comparisons but for programmatic direction-setting *within* the particular culture, our work may have significant meaning. For example, the American work ethic may be an emic that, while contributing to quality of life of people with disabilities in the United States, may not be so strongly valued in other cultures (Lobley, 1992). At the same time, notions about prejudice toward individuals with disabilities may be an etic that transcends the same cultural boundaries (Davies, 1986).

Our own experience to date suggests that the instruments we have studied are useful across cultures most readily when the cultures are more nearly similar. This conclusion is intuitively obvious and is borne out by work assessing the utility of our own questionnaires in the United Kingdom (Lobley, 1992; Rapley, 1994). This assessment was carried out with much less difficulty than our studies in Japan, where differences in language, cultural assumptions, and views of self present a much more difficult cross-cultural leap for American methodology.

Disabilities and Intercultural Quality of Life: Parallel Issues?

It has been argued that, for persons with mental retardation, assessment (if it is to be valid) must consider cultural and linguistic diversity in addition to behav-ioral and communicative issues (Luckasson et al., 1992). Further, test norms determined for one cultural group should not be exported to other cultural groups (Lonner, 1976). However, the concept of quality of life may present some special problems in this regard, to the extent that our aim, *within a par-ticular culture,* is in fact to compare a minority group (ethnic or disability) to the majority and to effect parity between the groups. For example, when Campbell, Converse, and Rodgers (1976) found lower life satisfaction among black Ameri-cans than among whites, it was logical to look at specific social and environmental differences that might be mitigated in order to reduce the discrepancy.

Likewise, when we find that citizens with mental retardation enjoy a lesser quality of life than their neighbors in the same town, we are likely to suggest that work needs to be done to improve their condition (Kixmiller, Keith, & Schalock, 1991)—not to argue that the measures should be rejected due to different normative standards. In this respect, the problems of individuals with disabilities may be similar to those of other cultural minorities—a possibility that I will attempt to illustrate by reference to some recently collected data.

One of my students, a native of Tonga, became interested in quality of life of Tongans living in the United States. As a result, we located 59 such individuals who were willing to complete the Quality of Life Questionnaire (Schalock & Keith, 1993). As we analyzed the data provided by these people, we began to see an interesting pattern: Although they were not persons with mental retarda-tion, their scores more nearly resembled those which we had collected from people with mild retardation than those of American adults without mental retardation. The total scores of the three groups are summarized in Table 8.1, along with subscale scores for the four factors assessed by the Questionnaire. It should be noted that all of the groups were of comparable ages (means in the range of 38 to 39 years).

Individuals with different backgrounds experience their worlds differently (Storti, 1994), a fact that our experience with these groups tended to confirm. Some of the Tongan respondents, for example, while seeing America as a land of great opportunity, were disillusioned to find that, for the first time in their lives, it was necessary to worry about money. Many of the obstacles they encounter are similar to those of people with mental retardation. If these groups are to achieve an acceptable quality of life in the American culture, it will be necessary for them and the culture to adapt in order to lessen the gaps between individual background (including previous cultural heritage) and current cultural expectations— perhaps an intercultural blending that allows a place for both the etic and the emic (Draguns, 1976). This is not the same issue, of course, as assessing the

quality of life of Tongans in Tonga; rather, it illustrates the special concerns inherent in intercultural adjustment within the diverse American cultural framework.

Some Guiding Principles

As we attempt to bring together the various issues involved in the understanding of cross-cultural measurement of quality of life, several central themes emerge that are likely to guide our work in the next few years.

1. Culture is not a clearly defined term. It is not defined by biology (that is, race) or by nationality. It is, rather, a construct involving shared values, beliefs, behaviors, and attitudes (Matsumoto, 1994). Individuals within a country (the U.S. is a good example) may well possess cultural characteristics that run counter to the dominant culture.

2. Although sensitivity to culture is essential, it is necessary to recognize that, in assessment of quality of life, as in other psychological processes (Draguns, 1976), it is the individual (and his or her perceptions) that

Table 8.1
Mean Scores on the Quality of Life Questionnaire for Three Cultural Subgroups

Quality of Life Subscale	Non-Tongan adults with mental retardation	Adults without mental retardation	
		Tongans	**Non-Tongans**
Satisfaction	22.7	23.5	25.1
Competence/Productivity	21.9	18.2	23.4
Empowerment/Independence	24.9	24.6	27.2
Social Belonging	22.5	23.9	24.1
Total Score	90.9	90.6	99.8

must remain the focus. This is not to suggest an individualistic rather than collective emphasis, but simply to indicate that, even in a collective culture, the *individual's* perception of happiness or satisfaction *in that context* remains paramount.

3. Comparative cross-cultural studies of quality of life, if their emphasis is evaluative, are likely to do little to advance our understanding of individual needs and wishes. Comparative studies that illuminate key characteristics of cultures and the quality of life of persons within them, on the other hand, are likely to contribute to cross-cultural understanding and communication in important ways.

4. We must recognize and overcome our propensity to project our own norms on people of other cultures. The pervasive and subtle nature of the manner in which we become culturally conditioned may cause us to believe that we (and hence everybody else) were simply born with a standard set of cultural behaviors (Storti, 1994), a mindset that will inevitably produce misunderstanding and miscommunication across cultures. It may be this tendency, at least in part, that causes Americans (and many others) to judge other cultures by American standards. This tendency is sometimes seen in assessments of programs serving individuals with mental retardation (Watanabe & Oshima, 1993). Such judgments are sometimes useful, but also carry the risk that we will overlay culturally inappropriate assumptions on the indigenous environment.

5. In investigating the concept of quality of life, the emphasis should be on our common humanity (Taylor & Bogdan, 1990). This means continued recognition of the point of view of the person, as well as respect for the subjective experience of the person—including the cultural and ethnic aspects of experience that have sometimes been trivialized or ignored by Western researchers (Lonner & Malpass, 1994).

I believe that Schalock et al. (1990) were right in suggesting that quality of life should be a guiding concept for international public policy, program practices, and cross-cultural research. Our challenge is to achieve these aims with sensitivity to, and in concert with, the ability of each individual to fully enjoy the context of his or her culture.

References

Abbey, A., & Andrews, F.M. (1986). Modeling the psychological determinants of life quality. In F.M. Andrews (Ed.), *Research on the quality of life* (pp. 85-116). Ann Arbor: The University of Michigan.

Beirne-Smith, M., Patton, J., & Ittenbach, R. (1994). *Mental retardation* (4th ed.). New York: Merrill.

Brislin, R. (1993). *Understanding culture's influence on behavior.* Fort Worth, TX: Harcourt Brace Jovanovich.

Campbell, A., Converse, P., & Rodgers, W.L. (1976). *The quality of American life: Perceptions, evaluations, and satisfactions.* New York: Russel Sage Foundation.

Campbell, A., & Kahn, R.L. (1976). Measuring the quality of life. In Commission on Critical Choices for Americans, *Qualities of life: Critical choices for Americans* (Vol. VII, pp. 163-187). Lexington, MA: Lexington Books.

Davies, N. (1986). *A comparative analysis of services for the mentally handicapped in Nebraska and Britain.* Unpublished thesis, University of Birmingham, Birmingham, England.

Draguns, J.G. (1976). Counseling across cultures: Common themes and distinct approaches. In P. Pedersen, W.J. Lonner, & J.G. Draguns (Eds.), *Counseling across cultures* (pp. 1-16). Honolulu: The University Press of Hawaii.

Feather, N.T. (1994). Values and culture. In W.J. Lonner and R. Malpass (Eds.), *Psychology and culture* (pp. 183-189). Boston: Allyn and Bacon.

Flanagan, J.C. (1978). A research approach to improving our quality of life. *American Psychologist, 33,* 138-147.

Flanagan, J.C. (1982). Measurement of quality of life: Current state of the art. *Archives of Physical Medicine and Rehabilitation, 63,* 56-59.

Goddard, H.H. (1912). *The Kallikak family.* New York: Macmillan.

Heal, L.W., Schalock, R.L., & Keith, K.D. (1992). *Cross-cultural attributions of meaning to quality of life concepts made by mental retardation professionals.* Paper presented at the meeting of the International Association for the Scientific Study of Mental Deficiency, Brisbane, Australia.

Keith, K.D., & Schalock, R.L. (1995). *Quality of student life questionnaire.* Worthington, OH: IDS Publishing Corp.

Keith, K.D., Yamamoto, M., Okita, N., & Schalock, R.L. (1995). Cross-cultural quality of life: Japanese and American college students. *Social Behavior and Personality, 23,* 163-170.

Kixmiller, J.S., Keith, K.D., & Schalock, R.L. (1991). Views on town and neighborhood: Adults with mental retardation and their neighbors. *Nebraska Journal of Psychology, 1,* 18-22.

Lobley, J. (1992). *Community living for people with learning disabilities: Is quality of life a useful guiding concept?* Unpublished thesis, Lancashire Polytechnic University, Preston, England.

Lonner, W.J. (1976). The use of Western-based tests in intercultural counseling. In P. Pedersen, W.J. Lonner, & J.G. Draguns (Eds.), *Counseling across cultures* (pp. 170- 183). Honolulu: The University Press of Hawaii.

Lonner, W.J., & Malpass, R.S. (1994). When psychology and culture meet: An introduction to cross-cultural psychology. In W.J. Lonner & R. Malpass (Eds.), *Psychology and culture* (pp. 1-12). Boston: Allyn and Bacon.

Luckasson, R., Coulter, D.L., Polloway, E.A., Reiss, S., Schalock, R.L., Snell, M.E., Spitalnik, D.M., & Stark, J.A. (1992). *Mental retardation: Definition, classification and systems of supports.* Washington, DC: American Association on Mental Retardation.

Markus, H., & Kitayama, S. (1991). Culture and the self: Implications for cognition, emotion, and motivation. *Psychological Review, 98,* 224-253.

Matsumoto, D. (1994). *People: Psychology from a cultural perspective.* Pacific Grove, CA: Brooks/Cole.

Myers, D.G. (1992). *The pursuit of happiness: Who is happy and why.* New York: William Morrow.

Potthoff, H.H. (1981). *Loneliness.* Denver: The Iliff School of Theology.

Rapley, M. (1994). *Factor analysis of the Schalock & Keith (1993) Quality of Life Questionnaire: A replication.* Unpublished manuscript, Lancaster University, Lancaster, England.

Schalock, R.L., Bartnik, E., Wu, F., Konig, A., Lee, C.S., & Reiter, S. (1990, May). *An international perspective on quality of life measurement and use.* Paper presented at the meeting of the Association on Mental Retardation, Atlanta, GA.

Schalock, R.L., & Keith, K.D. (1993). *Quality of life questionnaire.* Worthington, OH: IDS Publishing Corp.

Senoo, T. (1985). Introduction to welfare services for mentally retarded persons. *Services for people with mental retardation* (pp. 1-16). Tokyo: Japan League for the Mentally Retarded.

Storti, C. (1994). *Cross-cultural dialogues: 74 brief encounters with cultural difference.* Yarmouth, ME: Intercultural Press.

Taylor, S.J., & Bogdan, R. (1990). Quality of life and the individual's perspective. In R.L. Schalock (Ed.), *Quality of life: Perspectives and issues* (pp. 27-40). Washington, DC: American Association on Mental Retardation.

Tietjen, A.M. (1994). Children's social networks and social supports in cultural context. In W.J. Lonner & R. Malpass (Eds.), *Psychology and culture* (pp. 101-106). Boston: Allyn and Bacon.

Triandis, H.C. (1994). Culture and social behavior. In W.J. Lonner & R. Malpass (Eds.), *Psychology and culture* (pp. 169-173). Boston: Allyn and Bacon.

Watanabe, K., & Oshima, M. (1993). *Characteristics of social services for persons with intellectual disability in Japan—from some experiences in Thailand and Western countries.* Paper presented at the 11th Asian Conference on Mental Retardation, Seoul.

Wolff, M., Rutten, P., & Bayers, A.F. (1992). *Where we stand: Can America make it happen in the global race for wealth, health, and happiness?* New York: Bantam Books.

C H A P T E R   9

A Longitudinal-Ethnographic Research Perspective on Quality of Life

Robert B. Edgerton
University of California at Los Angeles

The assessment of the quality of one's life should occur within the context of a number of guiding principles that I discussed in the previous volume (Edgerton, 1990). Chief among these are the following:

- Although the quality of life can be measured by objective criteria, it is experienced subjectively.

- Providing improved objective standards of living does not necessarily increase peoples' sense of well-being.

- No single set of standards can possibly gratify all Americans.

- Individual choice should be the basis of any action taken on behalf of enhancing the quality of clients' lives.

- Persons with mental retardation must be encouraged to participate in program planning that involves quality of life issues.

The purpose of this chapter is to suggest that a longitudinal-ethnographic research perspective can be used to study the relationship experience of well-being. Major sections include a brief overview of longitudinal research on the quality of life, the description of an ethnographic approach, and a discussion of what our data have told us thus far about the relationship between changes in objective standards of life and subjective well-being.

A Longitudinal Perspective

As numerous reviews of the literature reporting longitudinal studies have noted, most of this body of research suffers from serious flaws of research design, with sampling and sample attrition being among the most common weaknesses (Bruininks, Meyers, Sigford, & Lakin, 1981; Heal, Sigelman, & Switsky, 1978; McCarver & Craig, 1974). Moreover, with a very few exceptions, this research reported on brief time spans, or if longer periods were considered, there were no more than two or three points of measurement (Cobb,

1972). Relatively continuous measurement over protected periods of time has rarely been attempted. Because measures of quality of life are inherently temporal, this lack is disappointing.

Even more disappointing for present purposes, this body of research tells us relatively little about changes in quality of life or subjective well-being. Few direct measures of either life quality or well-being are reported. Instead, reports concentrate on such findings as changes in marital, residential, vocational, or recreational patterns that, while certainly relevant to quality of life considerations, are relatively insensitive indicators of subjective well-being. For example, the 40-year follow-up of former special education students in San Francisco by Robert Ross and his associates (Ross, Begab, Dondis, Giampiccolo, & Meyers, 1985) painted an encouraging picture of the long-term community adaptation of these persons. We can see that these people have generally established lives that do not seem to differ greatly from those of their nonretarded relatives or peers. Yet we are told very little about the actual quality of those lives, the events that have had the greatest impact on these lives, or the feelings of the people themselves about their lives or themselves.

On balance, the longitudinal research available to us suggests that the majority of persons with mental retardation who are given an opportunity to live in community settings manage to achieve a reasonably successful adjustment to community living and that their adaptation tends to stabilize and improve over time. However, it also indicates that a minority—sometimes a sizable one— encounters serious difficulties in adapting to community living and returns to more restricted residential settings. It tells us very little about how these individual men and women search for friends and relationships, maintain their self-esteem, cope with their jobs or their joblessness, enjoy their leisure time, or worry about their futures. In short, we know all too little about the actual quality of their lives and next to nothing about their satisfaction with their lives. The voices of the people themselves have not been heard.

An Ethnographic Approach

In any effort to look more closely at the satisfaction of persons with mental retardation with their lives, it may be helpful to refer to some longitudinal research in which I have been involved. For the past 30 years, my colleagues and I have carried out longitudinal research using an ethnographic approach. Our ethnographic procedures require familiarity with as many aspects of a person's life as possible. Our methodological philosophy derives primarily from naturalism, rather than from positivistic behavioral science. We attempt to comprehend and interpret the phenomena under study as faithfully as possible; our goal is to be true to the phenomena themselves. We believe that such an interpretation can best be undertaken by following three principles (Edgerton & Langness, 1978):

- that phenomena be seen in their relevant context

- that these phenomena be seen not only through the observer's eyes, but those of the subject as well

- that reactive procedures be avoided at the same time that the investigator regards himself as a part of the phenomenon under investigation

No existing methodology for the study of human behavior adequately satisfies these three principles, and ours is no exception. Nevertheless, our procedures differ markedly from those commonly employed in the study of persons with mental retardation (interviews, tests, formal observation, self-reports, or second-hand accounts) and do, we believe, provide a useful perspective on persons' quality of life as well as their sense of well-being.

To carry out ethnographic naturalism, we must have prolonged contact with people. We must become, if only relatively so, a natural part of their lives. In time, we usually gain access to more than the public domain of their lives. We assume that people with mental retardation, like other people, manage their lives by saying and doing many things in order to present a favorable face to others. Our ethnographic procedures are sensitized to the Janus-faced quality of self-presentation, and by virtue of our prolonged and somewhat unpredictable presence in their world, we hope to be able to see more than the obvious. We often drop by unannounced, we take persons away from their residences to unfamiliar settings, and we talk to others about them. We attend important events in the lives of the people, going to weddings, family gatherings, or weekend outings, and we introduce them to new recreational experiences. Our procedures do not break down all deception (efforts to deceive are, after all, part of the reality we hope to study), nor do they reduce the complexities of human life to a clear and simple truth. However, the procedures do lessen the likelihood that an obvious deception will go unnoticed or that the contradictory complexity of a human life will be construed too simplistically. The method is not intended to provide simple answers; it is intended to provide the empirical grounds for rejecting simple answers in favor of fuller and more accurate understanding.

In time, people usually tell us how they feel about themselves and their lives. These expressions of satisfaction are not always consistent. Like the rest of us, people with mental retardation have good days and bad ones, and certain events or circumstances may evoke elation, anxiety, or depression. But over time the accumulation of naturally occurring statements combined with reactions to environmental changes usually allows us to make inferences about individuals' satisfaction with the quality of their lives that we believe are both reliable and valid. Words and deeds are not the same and need not be consistent, as we well know (Deutscher, 1966). Moreover, individuals often have positive and negative domains of affect that can express themselves independently of one another (Bradburn, 1969). But despite these complexities and contradictions, we believe that it is possible to reach valid conclusions about how satisfied most of the people we study are with their lives and what they would most like to change about those lives.

What Our Data Tell Us

The data that will be summarized here derive from longitudinal research with five principal samples: (a) 67 adults with retardation living in community residential facilities (Edgerton, 1975); (b) close to 100 clients of two large sheltered workshops (Zetlin & Turner, 1984); (c) 48 independently living young adults (Edgerton, 1981; Kaufman, 1984; Koegel, 1982); (d) 48 young Afro-Americans sampled to represent a range of independence and employability (Koegel & Edgerton, 1984; Mitchell-Kernan & Tucker, 1984); and (e) a sample of 48 (now reduced to 17) persons released from a large state institution over 30 years ago. With the exception of sample a, we have seldom gone more than a few months without being in contact with these people, and in some samples contact is more frequent than this.

It is neither possible nor appropriate to do more than briefly summarize the masses of data that have accumulated about the lives of these men and women. However, the findings and inferences that are reported here represent clear and pronounced patterns that have been observed by many of my colleagues and me for a number of years. First, one finding is quite clear: Younger people with retardation who are new to life in community settings are given to complaining about the lives they lead and their own self-esteem. They complain most often that they lack close relationships and, therefore, the opportunities to see themselves more positively that usually accompany reciprocal helping relationships. These complaints are well taken because, in truth, their lives are turbulent, and they give every evidence of being unhappy much of the time. Over time, these same people complain less and seem to become happier as their lives tend to stabilize. As these people grow older, they complain less and instead speak often about the rewards that their lives hold for them and strongly express their beliefs that the future will be at least as positive.

This pattern of growing confidence and satisfaction has been reported before (Edgerton, 1975) and may, therefore, be considered less than fully newsworthy. But if we turn from the kinds of group comparison analysis that led to this finding, to single-person-over-time analysis, another pattern emerges. When we track individuals over a period of 10, 15, or 30 years, a striking pattern of stability in their satisfaction with their lives emerges. As George (1979) has pointed out, we should first make a conceptual distinction between terms such as *happiness* (referring to transient affective states), *life satisfaction* (referring to how well life's expectations have been met), and *well-being* (a more global expression of satisfaction with the nature

and quality of one's life). The stability that we observe relates primarily to well-being, and secondarily so to life satisfaction. We find that major life events such as illness, loss of a loved one, or job loss can bring about changes in expressed life satisfaction and affect. But before long, people rebound and return to whatever state of global well-being they enjoyed before. In like fashion, some individuals enjoy sudden good fortune in the form of a new friendship, a better job, or an improvement in physical health, and respond with undisguised elation. However, in due course, they too return to their prior pattern of life satisfaction and well-being (Lazarus & Lannier, 1979).

Many have endured the death of loved ones, abandonment by friends or lovers, victimization such as rape, robbery, or assault, the loss of a job or a place to live, and life-threatening illness or surgery while remaining cheerful, satisfied with their lives, and optimistic about the future. But others, despite finding better jobs or places to live, making new friends, developing romantic attachments, and winning increased respect from friends or relatives, continue to complain about their lives, disparage themselves, and express fear that the future will be as bad, if not worse.

The pattern that emerges again and again is that people who were happy and hopeful 10, 20, or even 30 years ago remain so no matter what ill-fortune they suffer; and those who were sad or negative about life do not change even though their environment improves significantly. The data indicate clearly that major life stressors or gratifications can bring about changes in affect and expressed life satisfaction, but those changes are short lived.

Counterintuitive as this finding may seem to those like myself who believe in the causal power of environmental factors, these data suggest that internal dispositions—call them *temperament* for want of a better term—are better predictors of peoples' satisfaction with the quality of their lives than are objective environmental variables. If we take this finding seriously, it would have powerful implications for our ability to program an increased sense of well-being. Because it is such a controversial finding, one that tends to devalue environmental effects, we are obliged to ask whether there is any reason (other than my assertion) to believe that well-being may be relatively independent of objective standards of life's quality (Keogh & Pullis, 1980).

There are research reports from other populations that describe similar findings. Twenty years ago, Maddox (1968) reported that 148 noninstitutionalized persons age 60 and over showed substantial persistence in life-style patterns and well-being over the course of time, a finding that was replicated by other investigators who worked in the area of gerontology (Stones & Kozma, 1986). And Ormel (1983), examining data from a 6- to 7- year Dutch longitudinal study, concluded that how people respond to well-being measures over a period of years was primarily dependent on attributes of the persons, not on their environment. According to Ormel, neither deterioration nor improvement in life circumstances seemed to have had any significant effects on the amount of distress or satisfaction reported.

To further examine these challenging findings, let us turn to Costa, McCrae, and Zonderman (1987), who compared the responses given by 4,942 American men and women between 1981 and 1984 with responses these same people gave to the same questions a decade earlier. Subjects responded to 10 to 18 items in the General Well-Being Schedule (Dupuy, 1978); changes in life circum-

stances were inferred from current demographic data involving sex, race, age, income, education, and marital status, and therefore did not rely on subject's memory.

Because of this study's large and carefully selected stratified probability sample, its findings call for careful consideration. The authors reported that their data showed great stability in well-being measures over a 10-year interval. They asserted that they could predict future happiness more accurately from past measures of happiness than from age, sex, or race or from changes in marital status, work, or residence. They acknowledged that a large literature has reported that events like job loss, the death of a loved one, or divorce can have dramatic effects on well-being, but call attention to other studies (such as Palmore, Cleveland, Nowlin, Ramm, & Siegler, 1979) indicating that most people quickly adjust to such negative events. Moreover, as Brickman and Campbell (1971), Campbell, Converse, and Rodgers (1976), and others have shown, people adjust to improvements in their life circumstances even more rapidly.

There are limitations to the Costa et al. (1987) research. For example, it did not assess the effects of changes in health status on well-being, and its measure of well-being was so global that it could have missed more domain-specific effects of environmental change on well-being. And, in fact, there is evidence to suggest that well-being may be domain-specific—that is, residential well-being may be quite different from occupational well-being or marital well-being. Nevertheless, the possibility that a person's subjective sense of well-being may derive more from personal attributes than from the impact of his or her environment should not be rejected out of hand. There may be more than folk wisdom in the adage that "money can't buy happiness." Neither, perhaps, can changes in one's environment.

Conclusion

All of this speculation is intended as a cautionary note about the relationship between changes in objective standards of life and subjective well-being. Improving the quality of a person's life may increase his or her sense of well-being, or it may not. That remains an empirical question and a difficult one to answer. In my own view, it is likely that individuals differ greatly in their sensitivity to environmental effects. But let us suppose that the evidence I have summarized here is correct, and that features of a person's environment are less important in bringing about a sense of well-being than are aspects of that person's personality or temperament. If this finding were confirmed, what would that imply for our current and future efforts to ensure an improved quality of life for persons with mental retardation?

First, I believe that we must be prepared to uncouple objective standards of quality from the subjective experience of well-being. We should continue every effort to ensure that persons with mental retardation have access to better housing, health care, recreational activities, dignified employment, and everything else that an enlightened society can provide for its citizens. But we must never forget that all a society should do is provide options; however well-meaning, it should not impose standards. Nor should it imagine that all who accept its array of life-quality options will experience a greater sense of well-being than they did before, or that all who reject these options in favor of an alternative life-style will be less satisfied.

Because individual choice among available options is essential if there is to be any meaningful improvement in peoples' lives, we must assure that it is persons with mental retardation who choose what they want, not we who choose for them. And if their choices do not invariably bring them a greater sense of well-being, we should not then impose our choices on them. They, like the rest of us, should have the right to strive for satisfaction in life in their own way. And we must understand that some of them, like the rest of us, will be more successful than others.

References

Bradburn, N.M. (1969). *The structure of psychological well-being.* Chicago: Aldine.

Brickman, P., & Campbell, D.T. (1971). Hedonic relativism and planning the good society. In M.H. Appley (Ed.), *Adaptation level theory: A symposium.* New York: Academic Press.

Bruininks, R.H., Meyers, C.E., Sigford, B.B., & Lakin, K.C. (Eds.) (1981). *Deinstitutionalization and community adjustment of mentally retarded people* (Monograph No. 4). Washington, DC: American Association of Mental Deficiency.

Campbell, A., Converse, P.E., & Rodgers, W.L. (1976). *The quality of American life: Perceptions, evaluations, and satisfactions.* New York: Russell Sage Foundation.

Cobb, H. (1972). *The forecast of fulfillment: A review of research on predictive assessment of the adult retarded for social and vocational adjustment.* New York: Teachers College Press.

Costa, P.T., Jr., McCrae, R.R., & Zonderman, A.B. (1987). Environmental and dispositional influences on well-being: Longitudinal follow-up of an American national sample. *British Journal of Psychology, 78,* 299-306.

Deutscher, I. (1966). Words and deeds: Social science and social policy. *Social Problems, 13,* 235-254.

Dupuy, H.J. (1978, October). Self-representations of general psychological well-being of American adults. Paper presented at a meeting of the American Public Health Association, Los Angeles, CA.

Edgerton, R.B. (1975). Issues relating to the quality of life among mentally retarded persons. In M.J. Begab & S.A. Richardson (Eds.), *The mentally retarded and society: A social science perspective.* Baltimore: University Park Press.

Edgerton, R.B. (1981). Crime, deviance and normalization: Reconsidered. In R.H. Bruininks, C.E. Meyers, B.B. Sigford, & K.C. Lakin (Eds.), *Deinstitutionalization and community adjustment of mentally retarded people* (Monograph No. 4, pp. 169-174). Washington, DC: American Association of Mental Deficiency.

Edgerton, R.B. (1990). Quality of life from a longitudinal research perspective. In R.L. Schalock (Ed.), *Quality of life: Perspective and issues* (pp. 149-160). Washington, DC: American Association on Mental Retardation.

Edgerton, R.B., & Langness, L.L. (1978). Observing mentally retarded persons in community settings: An anthropological perspective. In G.P. Sackett (Ed.), *Observing behavior: Vol. I; Theory and applications in mental retardation* (pp. 210-219). Baltimore: University Park Press.

George, L.K. (1979). The happiness syndrome: Methodological and substantive issues in the study of social psychological well-being in adulthood. *The Gerontologist, 19,* 210-216.

Heal, L.W., Sigelman, C.K., & Switzky, H.N. (1978). Research in community residential alternatives for the mentally retarded. In N.R. Ellis (Ed.), *International review of research in mental retardation (Vol. 9)* (pp. 89-101). New York: Academic Press.

Kaufman, S. (1984). Friendship, coping systems and community adjustment of mildly retarded adults. In R.B. Edgerton (Ed.), *Lives in process: Mildly retarded adults in a large city* (Monograph No. 6, pp. 40-58). Washington, DC: American Association on Mental Deficiency.

Keogh, B.K., & Pullis, M.E. (1980). Temperament influences on the development of exceptional children. In B.K. Keogh (Ed.), *Advances in Special Education (Vol. 1),* (pp. 112-121). Greenwich, CT: JAI Press.

Koegel, P. (1982). Rethinking support systems: A qualitative investigation into the nature of social support. *Dissertation Abstracts International, 43,* 1214-A.

Koegel, P., & Edgerton, R.B. (1984). Black "six-hour retarded children" as young adults. In R.B. Edgerton (Ed.), *Lives in process: Mildly retarded adults in a large city* (Monograph No. 6, pp. 60-69). Washington, DC: American Association on Mental Deficiency.

Lazarus, R., & Lannier, R. (1979). Stress related transactions between person and environment. In L. Pervin & M. Lewis (Eds.), *Perspectives in international psychology* (pp. 142-156). New York: Plenum.

Maddox, G.I. (1968). Persistence of life style among the elderly: A longitudinal study of patterns of social activity in relation to life satisfaction. In B.I. Neugarten (Ed.), *Middle age and aging* (pp. 70-89). Chicago, IL: University of Chicago Press.

McCarver, R.B., & Craig, E.M. (1974). Placement of the retarded in the community: Prognosis and outcome. In N.R. Ellis (Ed.), *International review of research in mental retardation* (pp. 146-159). New York: Academic Press.

Mitchell-Kernan, C., & Tucker, M.B. (1984). The social structures of mildly mentally retarded Afro-Americans: Gender comparisons. In R.B. Edgerton (Ed.), *Lives in process: Mildly retarded adults in a large city* (Monograph No. 6, pp. 150-166). Washington, DC: American Association on Mental Deficiency.

Ormel, J. (1983). Neuroticism and well-being inventories: Measuring traits or states? *Psychological Medicine, 72,* 165-176.

Palmore, E.B., Cleveland, W.P., Jr., Nowlin, J.B., Ramm, D., & Siegler, I.D. (1979). Stress and adaptation in later life. *Journal of Gerontology, 34,* 841-851.

Ross, R.T., Begab, M.J., Dondis, E.H., Giampiccolo, J.S., Jr., & Meyers, C.E. (1985). *Lives of the mentally retarded: A forty year follow-up study.* Stanford, CA: Stanford University Press.

Stones, J.J., & Kozma, A. (1986). Happiness and activities as propensities. *Journal of Gerontology, 41,* 85-90.

Zetlin, A.G., & Turner, J.L. (1984). Self-perspectives on being handicapped: Stigma and adjustment. In R.B. Edgerton (Ed.), *Lives in process: Mildly retarded adults in a large city* (Monograph No. 6, pp. 180-194). Washington, DC: American Association on Mental Deficiency.

Methodological Issues in Quality of Life Measurement

Laird W. Heal
University of Illinois

Carol K. Sigelman
George Washington University

Although everyone seems to understand what is meant by quality of life, the meanings attached to this concept vary considerably. Moreover, the information investigators obtain about the quality of life of persons is intimately related to the ways in which they conceptualize and measure it. We leave to others (e.g., Goode, 1994; Heal, Borthwick-Duffy, & Saunders, 1995; Jamieson, 1993; Parent, 1992; Parmenter, 1992; Schalock, 1990) the formidable task of conceptualizing quality of life. Instead, we assume here that investigators know what they want to measure.

The purpose of this chapter is to help others decide how to measure it. Our purposes are to present some of the key methodological issues that arise in assessing quality of life and to offer some guidance about how to resolve them, drawing primarily on research that has systematically evaluated methodologies for interviewing both persons with and without mental retardation.

Fundamental Methodological Decisions

There are four major ways in which methodologies for assessing quality of life can differ.

1. Measures can be objective or subjective. That is, they can focus on the objective circumstances of people's lives (their income, housing, patterns of behavior, and so on) or they can assess attitudinal phenomena such as perceived satisfaction with life in general or with specific life circumstances. Objective measures can presumably be verified externally; subjective measures cannot.

2. A measure can be absolute or relative; it can directly index people's

quality of life or it can compare their quality of life to some standard such as what they would ideally want, what they experienced in the past, or what most other people experience.

3. Quality of life can be reported directly by the subjects of study or it can be assessed by someone else (by an informant or proxy such as a relative or friend, or by the investigators themselves, as when researchers record objective data or conduct behavioral observations).

4. The measure can be developed by the investigator or by the subjects of investigation. A subject-developed approach could entail using unstructured techniques such as participant observation to elucidate clients' own value systems and perspectives (e.g., Edgerton, 1975) or it could involve designing an instrument based on explicit input from subjects (as Flanagan, 1978, did after collecting data from some 3,000 people about specific critical incidents that had enhanced or worsened their lives).

Although this typology is by no means exhaustive, it serves to stimulate thinking about methodological choice points. Table 10.1 incorporates the four dimensions into a consideration of the what, who, and how of measuring quality of life. The what question concerns whether a measure assesses objective or subjective information and whether it assesses quality of life in an absolute or relative sense. The who question concerns whether individuals with mental retardation or other people develop the measures and provide the data. The how column reflects the more specific information goals and types of items that researchers select once they have made the fundamental decisions incorporated in the taxonomy. Finally,

the citations included in the table, drawn primarily but not exclusively from the mental retardation literature, offer a few examples of the approaches that have been used by quality of life researchers.

Most commonly, investigators themselves assess quality of life by employing investigator-generated measures (as Newton et al., 1988, have done by objectively assessing the number and types of activities in which clients engage) or they interview either clients or their proxies using investigator-generated interview schedules (as with the objective and subjective quality of life items created by Schalock and Keith, 1993). Other logical possibilities, such as client-developed objective measures that assess the objective life circumstances judged by individuals with mental retardation to be most central to their well-being, might prove to be very credible quality of life indicators.

The decisions implied by the taxonomy presented in Table 10.1 can have substantial effects on the information obtained. For example, different subjective measures of quality of life seem to reflect a single quality that has been labeled subjective well-being that correlates more highly with one another than they do with objective indices of quality of life (Andrews, 1986; Andrews & Withey, 1976; Diener, 1984). In other words, method variance tends to dominate substantive variance in quality of life assessments (Heal & Rubin, 1993). Moreover, many individuals seem to have difficulty responding to relative measures that require comparing current with past or future quality of life (Andrews & Withey, 1976). Indeed, Heal and Daniels (1986) developed such a relative quality of life measure for individuals with mental retardation but ultimately abandoned it because test-retest reliabilities were very low.

Table 10.1
Methodology Taxonomy for Assessing Quality of Life (QOL)

What?[a] General Method		Who? Respondent	Author	How?[b] Type of Instrument	Citation
Objective or Quasi-Objective	Absolute	Investigator	Investigator	Social interaction behaviors	Berkson & Romer (1980)
				Objective behavioral measures	Newton et al. (1988)
				Residence management styles	McLain et al. (1979)
				Quality of life items	Schalock & Keith (1993)
				Quality of care standards	Joint Commission on Accreditation of Healthcare Organizations
				Life safety codes	Feinstein (1985)
	Relative to some standard	Investigator	Investigator	Normalization relative to "cultural norms"	Wolfensberger & Thomas (1983)
Subjective	Absolute	Proxy	Investigator	Consumer satisfaction	Temple University DD Center and UAP (1988)
		Client	Investigator	Subjective well-being	Andrews & Withey (1976)
				Satisfaction with home, job, leisure	Heal, Harner, Amado, & Chadsey-Rusch (1993)
				QOL	Seltzer (1981)
			Client	Participant observation	Edgerton (1975)
				Evaluation of life's critical incidents	Flanagan (1978)
				Residents' perception of their homes	Moos (1975)
	Relative to some standard	Proxy	Investigator	-	-
		Client	Investigator	Relative subjective well-being	Heal & Daniels (1986)
			Client	-	-

[a]The questions of "where" and "when" are also methodologically critical, but they are not addressed in the current paper. "Where depends on the ecological validity (Bracht & Glass, 1968) requirements of the evaluation, and "when" depends upon the test-retest reliability requirements. [b]The type of instrument can also be classified by its item type: multiple choice, completion, open ended, open ended with examples, yes-no, Likert levels of agreement or disagreement, either-or—any of which can have pictures to make the questions less dependent on language.

The issue of who serves as respondent or data provider is also significant, particularly in assessing the quality of life of persons with mental retardation. For whatever reasons, answers provided by these individuals and answers provided by their parents or attendants sometimes disagree considerably (Sigelman et al., 1983). Although we know little about how findings based on investigator-developed and client-developed measures might differ, we can surmise that estimates of satisfaction with life circum- stances could differ substantially, depending on whether investigators or clients generate the list of specific life circumstances to be evaluated.

In short, investigations of quality of life can potentially rely on a wide range of fundamental methodologies. In practice, however, many of them have involved interviewing either individuals or their proxies. Accordingly, we now turn to the more specific methodological decisions that researchers face when interviewing people about their quality of life.

93

Factors Affecting Responses in Survey Research

In any research, validity of measurement must be established. In survey research, validity is diminished to the extent that "irrelevant" factors such as how a question is worded or who conducts the interview systematically alter the answers obtained. Those who would assess the quality of life of individuals with developmental disabilities can learn much from the literature on systematic response effects or sources of error in survey research (see Belson, 1986; Converse & Presser, 1986; Schuman & Presser, 1981; Turner, 1984). In a massive meta-analysis of such inadvertent response effects, Sudman and Bradburn (1974) reviewed and analyzed 935 references to methodological studies from 95 social science journals as well as numerous dissertations, monographs, and books. They directed attention to three broad classes of variable that can potentially alter or distort either objective or subjective survey data: task variables (for example, face-to-face vs. self-administered surveys, alternate question wordings); interviewer roles and characteristics; and respondent roles and characteristics.

Task Variables

Evidence suggests that responses can be systematically biased by question wording and question format or structure. For instance, Rugg (1941) asked these alternative questions: "Do you think the United States should allow public speeches against democracy?" and "Do you think the United States should forbid public speeches against democracy?" In response to the first question, 62% would not "allow" such speeches; in response to the second, only 46% would "forbid" such speeches. A seemingly minor difference in wording substantially altered responses.

Comparisons of closed-ended and open-ended questions reveal similar response effects associated with question format. Jenkins (1935) constructed an exhaustive checklist from all responses to a previously administered open-ended survey and found that this checklist (including an "all others" item) yielded response patterns closely comparable to those yielded by the open-ended survey. However, responses to an incomplete checklist, from which some of the popular answers had been removed, differed radically from responses to the open-ended question, suggesting that the specific make-up of a checklist, particularly its comprehensiveness, can greatly influence responding. When Belson and Duncan (1962) compared responses to checklist and open-ended questions about TV programs watched and periodicals read by respondents during a specified time period, the checklist yielded higher claims of activity, leading Belson (1986) to conclude that checklists are generally superior because they facilitate retrieval of information. However, a small fraction of respondents claimed to have watched programs included on the checklist that were not actually televised during the period of inquiry, suggesting that checklists can in some instances stimulate incorrect overreporting of behavior.

Survey researchers have also become sensitive to the fact that certain kinds of questions elicit systematic response biases. Questions that provide respondents with the opportunity to express agreement (by saying "yes," "true," "agree," and the like) may give rise to acquiescent responding. One strategy for detecting acquiescence is to ask content-free questions, as Gerjuoy and Winters (1966) did when they presented adults with mental retardation with pairs of identical geometric figures and asked if one of the figures was larger (or smaller). Of all responses, 59.1% were "yes," a departure from chance that reflects acquiescence. A second means of assessing acquiescence is to ask questions for which the correct answers are known. Thus, Cronbach (1942) discovered that students taking true-false tests were inclined to guess "true" when they were in doubt. Finally, acquiescence has been detected through item-reversal techniques in which a question and its opposite are asked and agreement with both questions indicates acquiescence. Using this approach in a study of children's cognitive development, Rothenberg (1969) discovered that fully 65% of the least cognitively mature children in the study contradicted themselves by saying that two sets of blocks had both the same number and a different number of blocks.

A related threat to validity is socially desirable responding, which is the tendency to present oneself in a favorable light (DeMaio, 1984). Scores on personality scales often correlate highly with the independently rated social desirability of scale items (Edwards, 1957). Similarly, many people respond to survey items in ways that suggest that they are concerned with obtaining social approval and are hesitant to admit to undesirable behaviors, especially when items are subjective or attitudinal, when it is obvious which options are socially desirable or undesirable, and when questions are presented in face-to-face interviews rather than in self-administered questionnaires (Sudman & Bradburn, 1974). Both social desirability and acquiescence have proven to be significant problems in quality of life research, perhaps helping to explain why members of the general population typically rate the quality of their lives above the neutral point, regardless of

how neutral is anchored or described (Andrews & Withey, 1976; Diener, 1984).

Three other messages about the effects of task variables on survey responses are worth mentioning. First, when respondents are asked to recall behavioral information, particularly about socially disapproved activities, their tendency to underreport behaviors increases as the length of the recall period lengthens (Sudman & Bradburn, 1974). Second, responses to particular questions can vary depending on the context in which they appear. For example, people report higher levels of general happiness when they have just been asked about their marital happiness than when they have just been asked about their finances (Turner, 1984). Finally, the ranges of such response effects or biases are larger for attitudinal (subjective) questions than for behavioral (objective) questions.

Interview Variables

Sudman and Bradburn (1974) concluded that response effects attributable to interviewer characteristics such as age, sex, race, and social class are generally less powerful than those attributable to task variables. When interviewer characteristics do matter, it is usually under highly specific conditions such as the interviewer's race influencing responses when people are asked about their racial attitudes (Schuman & Converse, 1971).

Respondent Variables

Sudman and Bradburn (1974) concluded that the strength of response biases generally did not vary as a function of the gender, race, or age of the respondent. However, they did find that children with 8 years or less of school tended to be especially susceptible to many response effects. Moreover, respondent and task variables sometimes interact. For example, elementary school students are especially likely to overreport their behavior in response to closed-ended checklists, and respondents with less than a high school education are especially likely to give different answers to long questions than to short questions. Although Sudman and Bradburn generally did not find level of education to be an influential factor within the adult population, Schuman and Presser (1977; 1981) have found that adults with limited education are especially susceptible to certain response effects. Specifically, compared with more educated adults, they are especially likely to acquiesce, to give discrepant answers to "allow" versus "forbid" question wordings, and to underreport on open-ended questions but overreport on closed-ended questions.

Implications for Interviewing Persons with Mental Retardation

The response effects literature carries some sobering messages for those who would assess the quality of life of individuals with mental retardation. It clearly demonstrates that variations in such task factors as question wording, question structure or format, and the extent to which a question implies a socially desirable response can alter the answers provided by individuals without retardation. Fortunately, this literature contains many practical guidelines about how to minimize response effects and write effective questions (Andrews & Withey, 1976; Converse & Presser, 1986; Sudman & Bradburn, 1982). Tactics that increase validity of response in the general population (including individuals who serve as proxies) are also likely to increase response validity. However, one must still expect that questioning respondents with mental retardation about their quality of life will raise some

unique methodological problems. Thus, there is ultimately no substitute for systematic research on the ability of individuals with mental retardation to answer questions and to answer them meaningfully. We now turn to that research.

Research on Interviewing Persons with Mental Retardation

Most of the fairly small body of research on the methodology of interviewing persons with mental retardation was conducted at the Research and Training Center in Mental Retardation at Texas Tech University (see Sigelman, Winer, Schoenrock, & Martin, 1982). The project involved administering 20- to 30-minute interviews containing alternative forms of questions, presenting the same or alternative questions in repeated interviews approximately one week apart, and conducting parallel interviews with parents or direct care staff to determine the extent of agreement between interviewees and informants speaking on their behalf.

Four standards were applied in judging which of various alternative questions were the most promising as approaches to obtaining meaningful information directly from persons with mental retardation: responsiveness (the proportion of interviewees who could answer a question, regardless of the truth or falsity of answers); test-retest reliability (correspondence between answers to the same questions on two occasions); consistency (correspondence between responses to questions whose wording or format differed but whose meaning remained the same); and agreement with informants or, in some instances, with objective fact.

Responsiveness

Sigelman, Winer, and Schoenrock (1982) found that high proportions (generally over 80%) of their samples could provide answers to yes-no questions (e.g., "Do you set the table?") and to picture-choice questions (e.g., given four face drawings ranging from very happy to very sad, "Which picture shows how you like the food here?"). Yes-no questions about activities tended to be easier to answer than yes-no questions about subjective phenomena such as happiness. Verbal either-or questions were answerable by 66% to 72% of the three main samples, and verbal multiple choice questions and open-ended questions proved to be the most cognitively demanding, answerable by about half of the institutionalized respondents and 70% of the community children. Responsiveness to questions increased as IQ increased (Sigelman et al., 1980).

Reliability

The test-retest reliability figures reported by Sigelman et al. (1983) are both gratifying and disappointing. For example, when children who were institutionalized were asked the same yes-no questions about their activities on two occasions about a week apart, their answers were consistent an average of 87% of the time. However, this estimate of reliability was inflated by the strong tendency to say "yes" to most questions. What may have been reliable was the tendency to acquiesce rather than the tendency to provide valid information. Four-option multiple choice questions about activities, although answerable by relatively few individuals, yielded about 72% test-retest agreement; whereas the consistency of answers to multiple choice questions presenting four levels of happy and sad faces and inquiring about satisfaction with living circumstances was discouragingly low (46%).

Open-ended questions about discrete facts were answered consistently about two-thirds of the time (e.g., 63% gave the same first and last names on both occasions when asked their name), but open-ended questions calling for enumerations of activities only rarely yielded mention of the same activity both times and had high reliability only in the sense that many activities were *not* mentioned both times. Although these reliability estimates suggest that one can usually get the same answer from individuals with retardation on two occasions, reliability estimates are difficult to interpret without determining whether the answers obtained also seem to be valid.

Consistency

Perhaps the most compelling criterion of the adequacy of a questioning approach is that it yield answers that are consistent with answers to alternative questions on the same topics and that are relatively free of systematic response bias. The Texas Tech data demonstrate that acquiescence in response to yes-no questions is a major source of response inconsistency (e.g., Sigelman, Budd, Spanhel, & Schoenrock (1981). In fact, substantial acquiescence has been found in respondents with mental retardation by Harner (1991; 35%); Heal and Chadsey-Rusch (1985; 55%); Heal and Rubin (1993; 50%); and Novak, Heal, Pilewski, and Laidlaw (1989; 35%). It may well be that persons with mental retardation may say yes to many yes-no questions in order to be agreeable *and* may say no to questions that mention socially undesirable behaviors to deny any association with these taboos (Heal & Sigelman, in press).

Although the problem of acquiescence in response to yes-no questions can be severe, either-or questions sometimes engendered a systematic response bias of their own (Sigelman et al., 1981).

When asked parallel either-or questions in which only the order of options was altered (e.g., "Are you usually happy or sad?" "Are you usually sad or happy?"), respondents were more likely to contradict themselves by choosing the second option both times. This recency bias was fairly prevalent, characterizing an average of almost 21% of paired answers in three samples.

Noting that none of these studies had completely separated the form of the question from the information that it was designed to uncover, Heal and Rubin (1993) made the two orthogonal in a factorial (format by content) analysis of variance design. They asked 91 adults with mental retardation about their satisfaction with six aspects of their lives: home, job, friends, free time, favorite food, and favorite activity. Each respondent was asked to indicate their satisfaction with each domain by responding to 12 variations (formats) of the same question. Consistent with prior findings, 50% acquiescence bias was found on reverse worded yes-no questions, and 10% recency bias on reverse-worded either-or questions.

Finally, open-ended questions were associated with the response bias of underreporting activities. As a result of both underreporting on open-ended questions and acquiescing on yes-no questions, respondents typically claimed to engage in far fewer activities when they were asked open-ended questions than when they were asked yes-no questions (Sigelman, Winer, & Schoenrock, 1982). Although Belson (1986) concluded that yes-no checklists are preferable to open-ended questions in surveys of the general population, either approach is suspect with respondents who are mentally retarded.

Interestingly, just as practice in answering questions seems to improve

responsiveness to questions (Sigelman et al., 1983), it may also improve consistency of response to alternative questions. Conroy and Bradley (1985) found that only 16 of 23 residents of an institution responded consistently to a yes-no question and a multiple-choice question with happy and sad faces about satisfaction with their living circumstances. Four years later, deinstitutionalized individuals responded with perfect consistency. While this increase in consistency may have been attributable more to the respondent's strong preference for remaining in the community than to their considerable experience in being interviewed, residents who remained in the institution also displayed substantial increases in response consistency on various satisfaction items over time.

Agreement with Informants or Factual Records

The final standard that was applied by Sigelman et al. (1983) in judging the quality of information received from interviewees with mental retardation was its agreement with information obtained from other sources. While one should not assume that disagreements between individuals with retardation and their parents or direct care staff necessarily reflect invalid responding, one can be more confident of responses if two respondents agree. In one fairly representative analysis of resident-staff agreement, agreement was 52% for a yes-no checklist and 60% for an open-ended question about participation in various sports (Budd, Sigelman, & Sigelman, 1981). Disagreements in response to the checklist most often involved the resident's saying "yes" but the caretaker's saying "no," whereas disagreements on the open-ended question more often involved the resident's not mentioning an activity that the caretaker mentioned. This pattern of disagreements suggested that acquiescence and underreporting on the part of individuals with mental retardation were largely, although not totally, responsible for discrepancies between their answers and the answers provided by care staff. At the same time, correlations between IQ and agreement, while significant in two of three samples, were weaker than one might expect (Sigelman et al., 1980), implying that agreement with informants is an imperfect indicator of response validity.

Yet the validity of answers obtained is often limited even when the standard of validity is known. Many individuals have difficulty providing accurate responses to open-ended questions inquiring about their full names, birthdates, and addresses (Sigelman et al., 1983). Some cannot answer such questions, and about a third of those who do answer do not provide fully correct information.

Possible Solutions

Perhaps the main message of this research is that obtaining meaningful information about quality of life directly from individuals with mental retardation is problematic. Simply getting answers from individuals with limited verbal skills is only the first of the challenges. Response effects that jeopardize the validity of answers obtained from the general population seem to operate even more strongly in persons with mental retardation. Where does this leave researchers who wish to survey persons with mental retardation about their quality of life? Let's consider three alternatives.

Identify Optimally Effective Questioning Techniques

The solution adopted by the Texas Tech researchers was to identify optimally effective questioning techniques by pitting alternative questions against each other and determining which of them optimized responsiveness, reliability, self-consistency, and agreement with informants or known facts. By these criteria, either-or questions (or objective multiple-choice questions with three or four options accompanied by pictures) surfaced as the most promising questioning approach. Factual multiple-choice questions offering discrete options (ways to get to school or types of dwellings) worked well, much better than multiple-choice questions presenting happy and sad faces or quantitative options such as a lot, sometimes, not much, and never (Sigelman et al., 1983). Moreover, when Sigelman and Budd (1986) systematically compared questions with and without pictures, they found that pictures enhanced responsiveness to either-or and multiple-choice questions, only slightly reduced agreement with informants, and, particularly in the low verbal sample, reduced the tendency to choose the second of the two options in either-or questions. Thus, instead of using a yes-no checklist to find out about participation in various activities, one might develop line drawings of these activities, a comparison drawing of a person doing nothing, and ask questions like this: "Some people cook their dinner on the stove. Other people don't cook their dinner on the stove. Which one is most like you? Point to the picture." Such questions, especially when they are objective rather than subjective, can be answered by most persons and, more importantly, can yield relatively valid answers.

Correct Statistically for Response Bias

A second approach, adopted by Heal and Chadsey-Rusch (1985), is to interview individuals with whatever types of questions seem most natural and then statistically correct for response bias. In their 29-item Lifestyle Satisfaction Scale, they included an acquiescence subscale, which consisted of paired questions for which responding yes to both would constitute self-contradiction and indicate acquiescence. Using multiple regression techniques, life-style satisfaction scores were then corrected for acquiescence (adjusted downward, because acquiescence predictably inflated estimates of satisfaction). This approach has considerable promise, and it could also be used to adjust either-or measures for the recency or second option response bias.

Use Proxies

A third option is to concede that many persons with mental retardation cannot provide meaningful information in interviews and to rely instead on data provided by informants or by the investigators themselves. A less extreme variant of this solution is to devise a screening interview that can be used to determine whether the individual or someone else should provide quality of life data. Such a screening interview might assess responsiveness to questions, determine the validity of responses to basic questions whose answers are known, and gauge susceptibility to response biases that might compromise the validity of answers to the full interview. The problem, of course, is that any resulting differences in quality of life between higher-ability and lower-ability individuals might be attributable more to the different research methods used than to true differences in the quality of their lives.

Ultimately, researchers might do best to adopt a blend of these approaches. For example, they might rely on either-or or multiple-choice questions accompanied by pictures whenever feasible; build into their interview schedules checks for response bias that can later be used to adjust scores to remove the effects of response bias; and turn to information-gathering techniques other than client interviews when those alternative techniques are likely to yield the most valid data.

Summary and Conclusions

We began this chapter by presenting several fundamental methodological decisions that must be made in order to assess the quality of life of persons with mental retardation, calling attention to potentially important distinctions between objective and subjective, absolute and relative, subject-completed and informant-completed, and subject-generated and investigator-generated measures. We then turned to some of the methodological problems that arise in interviewing, particularly problems stemming from systematic response biases associated with question format and wording. The literature in this area clearly demonstrates that what one learns about the quality of life of individuals without retardation can differ considerably depending on how questions are asked. This means, of course, that information obtained from individuals who serve as proxies for individuals with retardation cannot be assumed to be valid unless care is taken in designing survey instruments to reduce response effects.

The challenges of assessing quality of life through survey methods are only magnified when individuals with mental retardation serve as respondents. It seems challenging indeed to get answers to questions from many persons with mental retardation and, more importantly, to elicit responses that are reliable, consistent with responses to different questions on the same topic, and substantiated by information obtained from other sources. These rather discouraging findings may tempt researchers to forgo interviewing persons with mental retardation entirely. Thus, investigator-gathered behavioral observations of rates of smiling, laughing, frowning, and crying might be used in place of self-reports of subjective well-being.

Our own position is that multiple methodologies, each of them demonstrated to be reliable and valid, are needed in order to adequately assess quality of life, and that interviews with consumers of mental retardation services should be one of these methodologies. There are compelling philosophical reasons for providing consumers with opportunities to tell us how they perceive their lives and how they would like their lives to change. Moreover, we have directed attention in this chapter to empirically-based guidelines that can improve survey methodology and enable more individuals to speak for themselves. For interviews to yield useful information, researchers must seek information as effectively as current technology permits. Developing *any* reliable and valid quality-of-life measure requires considerable effort, effort that promises to result in a fuller understanding of the lives of persons with mental retardation.

Author Note

This report was supported in part by the Office of Special Education and Rehabilitative Services, U.S. Department of Education, under a contract (300-85-0160) to the Transition Research Institute at the University of Illinois.

References

Andrews, F.M. (Ed.). (1986). *Research on the quality of life.* Ann Arbor: University of Michigan.

Andrews, F.M., & Withey, S.B. (1976). *Social indicators of well-being: Americans' perceptions of life quality.* New York: Plenum.

Belson, W.A. (1986). *Validity in survey research.* Brookfield, VT: Gower Publishing.

Belson, W.A., & Duncan, J.A. (1962). A comparison of the checklist and the open response questioning systems. *Applied Statistics, 11,* 120-132.

Berkson, G., & Romer, D. (1980). Social ecology of supervised communal facilities for mentally disabled adults: I. Introduction. *American Journal of Mental Deficiency, 85,* 219-228.

Bracht, G.H., & Glass, G.V. (1968). The external validity of experiments. *American Educational Research Journal, 5,* 437-474.

Budd, E.C., Sigelman, C.K., & Sigelman, L. (1981). Exploring the outer limits of response bias. *Sociological Focus, 14,* 297-307.

Conroy, J.W., & Bradley, V.J. (1985). *The Pennhurst longitudinal study.* Philadelphia: Developmental Disabilities Center, Temple University.

Converse, J.M., & Presser, S. (1986). *Survey questions: Handcrafting the standardized questionnaire* (Sage University Paper Series, Quantitative Applications in the Social Sciences No. 07-063). Beverly Hills: Sage.

Cronbach, L.J. (1942). Studies of acquiescence as a factor in the true-false test. *Journal of Educational Psychology, 33,* 401-415.

DeMaio, T.J. (1984). Social desirability and survey measurement: A review. In C.F. Turner & E. Martin (Eds.), *Surveying subjective phenomena (Vol. 2)* (pp. 257-282). New York: Russell Sage.

Diener, E. (1984). Subjective well-being. *Psychological Bulletin, 95,* 542-575.

Edgerton, R.B. (1975). Issues relating to the quality of life among mentally retarded persons. In M.J. Begab & S.A. Richardson (Eds.), *The mentally retarded and society: A social science perspective.* Baltimore: University Park Press.

Edwards, A.L. (1957). *The social desirability variable in personality assessment and research.* New York: Dryden Press.

Feinstein, C.A. (1985). *Life safety code instrument.* Philadelphia: Conroy and Feinstein Associates.

Flanagan, J.C. (1978). A research approach to improving our quality of life. *American Psychologist, 33,* 138-147.

Gerjuoy, I., & Winters, J.J., Jr. (1966). Lateral preference for identical geometric forms: II. Retardates. *Perception & Psychophysics, 1,* 104-106.

Goode, D. (1994). *Quality of life for persons with disabilities.* Cambridge, MA: Brookline Books.

Harner, C. (1991). *Assessing the satisfaction of adults with mental retardation living in the community.* Unpublished doctoral dissertation, University of Illinois, Urbana, IL.

Heal, L.W., Borthwick-Duffy, S., & Saunders, R.R. (1995). Assessment of quality of life. In J.W. Jacobson & J.A. Mulick (Eds.) *Manual of diagnosis and professional practice in mental retardation.* Washington, DC: American Psychological Association.

Heal, L.W., & Chadsey-Rusch, J. (1985). The lifestyle satisfaction scale (LSS): Assessing individuals' satisfaction with residence, community setting, and associated services. *Applied Research in Mental Retardation, 6,* 475-490.

Heal, L.W., & Daniels, B.S. (1986). A cost-effectiveness analysis of residential alternatives for selected developmentally disabled citizens of three northern Wisconsin counties. *Mental Retardation Systems, 2,* 35-49.

Heal, L.W., Harner, C., Amado, A.R.N., & Chadsey-Rusch, J. (1993). *The lifestyle satisfaction scale.* Worthington, OH: IDS Publishing Co.

Heal, L.W., & Rubin, S.S. (1993, May). *Biases in responses during interviews of individuals with mental retardation.* Paper presented at the annual meeting of the American Association on Mental Retardation, Washington, DC.

Heal, L.W., & Sigelman, C.K. (in press). Response biases in interviews of individuals with limited mental ability. *Journal of Intellectual Disability Research.*

Jamieson, J. (1993). *Adults with mental handicap: Their quality of life.* Vancouver, BC: British Columbia Ministry of Social Services.

Jenkins, J. (1935). *Psychology in business and industry.* New York: Wiley.

Joint Commission on the Accreditation of Healthcare Organizations. (1995). *Accreditation manual for mental health, chemical dependency, mental retardation, and other developmental disabilities services.* Chicago, IL: Author.

McLain, R.E., Silverstein, A.B., Hubbell, M., Brownless, L., Sutter, P., & Mayeda, T. (1979). *The residential management survey.* Pomona, CA: Riverside Research Group at Lanterman Developmental Center.

Moos, R.H. (1975). *Evaluating correctional and community settings.* New York: Wiley.

Newton, S., Bellamy, G.T., Boles, S.M., Stoner, S., Horner, R., LeBaron, N., Moskowitz, D., Romer, M., & Schlessinger, D. (1988). *Valued outcomes information system (VOIS) operations manual.* Eugene: University of Oregon, Center on Human Development.

Novak, A.R., Heal, L.W., Pilewski, M.B., & Laidlaw, T. (1989, May). *Apartment placement from a community ICFMR.* San Francisco: Annual meeting of the American Association on Mental Retardation.

Parent, W. (1992). Quality of life and consumer choice. In P. Wehman (Ed.), *ADA mandate for social change* (pp. 19-41). New York: Academic Press.

Parmenter, T.R. (1992). Quality of life for people with developmental disabilities. In N.W. Bray (Ed.), *International review of research in mental retardation (Vol. 18)* (pp. 247-287). New York: Academic Press.

Rothenberg, B. (1969). Conversation of number among four- and five-year old children: Some methodological considerations. *Child Development, 40,* 382-406.

Rugg, D. (1941). Experiments in wording questions: II. *Public Opinion Quarterly, 5,* 91-92.

Schalock, R.L. (Ed.) (1990). *Quality of life: Perspectives and issues.* Washington, DC: American Association on Mental Retardation.

Schalock, R.L., & Keith, K.D. (1993). *Quality of life questionnaire.* Worthington, OH: IDS Publishing Co.

Schuman, H., & Converse, J.M. (1971). The effects of black and white interviewers on white respondents in 1968. *Public Opinion Quarterly, 35,* 44-68.

Schuman, H., & Presser, S. (1977). Question wording as an independent variable in survey analysis. *Sociological Methods and Research, 6,* 151-170.

Schuman, H., & Presser, S. (1981). *Questions and answers in attitude surveys: Experiments on question form, wording, and context.* New York: Academic.

Seltzer, G.B. (1981). Community residential adjustment: The relationship among environment, performance, and satisfaction. *American Journal of Mental Deficiency, 85,* 624-630.

Sigelman, C.K., & Budd, E.C. (1986). Pictures as an aid in questioning mentally retarded persons. *Rehabilitation Counseling Bulletin, 29,* 173-181.

Sigelman, C.K., Budd, E.C., Spanhel, C.L., & Schoenrock, C.J. (1981). Asking questions of retarded persons: A comparison of yes-no and either-or formats. *Applied Research in Mental Retardation, 2,* 347-357.

Sigelman, C.K., Budd, E.C., Winer, J.W., Schoenrock, C.J., & Martin, P.W. (1982). Evaluating alternative techniques of questioning mentally retarded persons. *American Journal of Mental Deficiency, 86,* 511-518.

Sigelman, C.K., Schoenrock, C.J., Budd, E.C., Winer, J.L., Spanhel, C.L., Martin, P.W., Hromas, S., & Bensberg, G.J. (1983). *Communicating with mentally retarded persons: Asking questions and getting answers.* Lubbock: Texas Tech University, Research and Training Center in Mental Retardation.

Sigelman, C., Schoenrock, C., Spanhel, C., Hromas, S., Winer, J., Budd, E., & Martin, P. (1980). Surveying mentally retarded persons: Responsiveness and response validity in three samples. *American Journal of Mental Deficiency, 84,* 479-486.

Sigelman, C.K., Winer, J.L., & Schoenrock, C.J. (1982). The responsiveness of mentally retarded persons to questions. *Education and Training of the Mentally Retarded, 17,* 120-124.

Sudman, S., & Bradburn, N.M. (1974). *Response effects in surveys: A review and synthesis.* Chicago, IL: Aldine.

Sudman, S., & Bradburn, N.M. (1982). *Asking questions: A practical guide to questionnaire design.* San Francisco: Jossey-Bass.

Temple University Developmental Disabilities Center and University Affiliated Program (1988). *A national survey of consumers of services for individuals with developmental disabilities.* Philadelphia: Temple University.

Turner, C.F. (1984). Why do surveys disagree? Some preliminary hypotheses and some disagreeable examples. In C.F. Turner & E. Martin (Eds.), *Surveying subjective phenomena (Vol. 2),* (pp. 159-214). New York: Russell Sage.

Wolfensberger, W., & Thomas, S. (1983). *PASSING (program analysis of service systems implementation of normalization goals): Normalization criteria and ratings manual* (2nd Ed.). Toronto: National Institute on Mental Retardation.

Evaluation and Measurement of Quality of Life: Special Considerations for Persons with Mental Retardation

Sharon A. Borthwick-Duffy

University of California, Riverside

When the concept of quality of life first attracted attention in the field of mental retardation, Landesman challenged professionals to seriously consider the implications of using quality of life criteria in policies and service-related decisions. Among her recommendations were the following: to determine what was meant by the term "quality of life," to develop ways of evaluating and measuring this construct, and to identify variables in environments that were associated with a better quality of life (Landesman, 1986).

Landesman's admonishment was based on a realization that quality of life measures would become the basis of important decisions made on behalf of persons with mental retardation, and that these decisions could only be made responsibly if the above challenges were addressed. As expected, quality of life has shifted in the last decade from being primarily a topic of academic discourse,

often focusing on issues related to the dimensional structure and subjective versus objective perspectives, to playing a vital role in decisions that have a major impact on people's lives. Hence, given that quality of life has become a central theme in the planning and evaluation of services for people with mental retardation, it is fitting that this chapter review the progress that has been made in relation to the conceptualization and assessment of the construct, as well as the knowledge gained about contextual factors that have been found to be associated with a better quality of life. This chapter begins with a discussion of ways in which the consideration of quality of life can significantly impact the lives of people with mental retardation. Then, given its increasingly important role, the chapter addresses topics that influence the way quality of life is defined and measured.

Quality of Life Evaluations Have Serious Consequences

Beyond success and failure: A closer look at placement decisions.

Considerations of quality of life criteria in residential, educational, and vocational placement decisions have forced service providers and families to gauge "success" in placements by more than just stability or lack of recidivism to more restrictive settings (formerly labelled "failure"). Whereas a focus on the extent to which settings were considered "normalized" represented the first move away from the success/failure dichotomy, recent attention to the life conditions of individuals in those settings has been consistent with efforts to also consider more subtle, but important indicators of "quality of life," "happiness," or "satisfaction" (Schalock, 1990). In other words, decisions about programs and placements are now based on the assumption that a setting will provide the individual with the best quality of life.

Current trends that emphasize total integration with nonhandicapped peers in educational settings (full inclusion), vocational settings (competitive employment), and residential placement (independent living) are based on a presumed positive relationship between high levels of integration with people without disabilities and a higher quality of life. But the fact that many professionals once had different views of this relationship (i.e., that segregated settings provided *more positive* experiences and led to *better* outcomes) highlights the potential impact of our assumptions about quality of life and its measurement on service delivery and eventual outcomes for people with mental retardation. When particular services or placements are thought to lead to a better quality of life, those services are valued, and decisions made by professionals reflect these values.

Use of quality of life estimates to deny opportunities.

Quality of life considerations have not always led to positive outcomes for people with mental retardation and other severe disabilities. Baroff (1986) concluded, for example, that the existence of mental retardation has been a relevant factor in the determination of quality of life requirements, sometimes leading to lowered expectations and denial of opportunities. For people with disabilities, quality of life is both a matter of definition and *entitlement,* i.e., "what minimal advantages are persons with mental retardation entitled to both as human beings and as individuals with handicaps" (Rosen, 1986, p. 365). Medical treatment is a good example of mental retardation influencing decisions about entitlements. Over the years, quality of life criteria have furnished a rationale for deciding whether to provide medical treatment to people with mental retardation, as illustrated in the following two sections.

Use of quality of life estimates to justify involuntary euthanasia.

Quality of life has been used as a basis for making ethical decisions about who should live and who should die. Lusthaus (1985) referred to a "quality of life perspective" as the most common approach used in attempting to define personhood (or lack of), and thus determine whether an individual is able to have a meaningful existence:

> *Lives that are not worthwhile are thought to be less than fully human, for fully human lives have potential worth. Many people who have mental retardation would be seen as having meaningless lives by the quality of life standards,*

and would fall into the nebulous species of nonhuman.

(pp. 149-150)

According to this view, those who are judged to be "nonhuman" would be better off if they had not lived. This position has been cited as the basis for withholding medical treatment to infants and children (e.g., Baby Doe); in the absence of a severe disability, treatment would have otherwise been considered routine. Although Lusthaus characterized euthanasia based on the quality of life perspective as murder, she cited numerous instances in which government and professional organizations had considered quality of life as an important criterion for setting ethical policies about treatment of individuals with severe mental retardation (Lusthaus, 1985).

Policies based on quality of life assume there is a common interpretation of human "worth" or of a meaningful life. Powell and Hecimovic (1985) disagree with this assumption. First, they discuss problems with identification of the important dimensions of quality of life:

The term "quality of life" lends itself to a rather subjective and possibly biased definition. It is unsettling that critical decisions may be based on so loosely analyzed a concept. Without a full understanding of the relevant dimensions of a quality of life, we may be forestalling our full understanding of the attainment of that goal by persons with severe handicaps.

(pp. 316-317)

The second point made by Powell and Hecimovic relates to whether the *right* to life should be weighed against the potential *quality* of that life. In their view, euthanasia based on a quality of life rationale will "impede present and future research efforts aimed at improving quality of life" (p. 321) if these individuals are denied their right to live. They provide convincing evidence that the quality of life perspective is often used to support involuntary euthanasia involving infants, by rescuing them from what is considered a meaningless existence.

Quality of life as a basis for allocating government funded treatments. A second example of quality of life estimates leading to negative outcomes focuses on government funding of treatment for medical conditions. Stade (1993) described a recent proposal to ration state-funded medical treatment. Ratings were solicited from 1,001 citizens regarding the estimated effect of 709 medical symptoms on the quality of their lives. Each condition was then assigned units of "quality of well-being." The ranks were used to determine which residents living in poverty could be treated at state expense for their medical problems. The drawback to this method was that some medical conditions that were likely to occur more often among persons with developmental disabilities received lower rankings. Critics claimed that the method associated quality of life with the absence of a disability, and valued people without disabilities more highly than people with disabilities in the allocation of medical treatment. This case again illustrates the powerful effect quality of life estimates can have on services provided or denied to people with mental retardation.

Definition Precedes Quantification

Evaluation and measurement of quality of life requires that conceptual models be operationalized in some way. Differences in models and in assumptions regarding quality of life can lead to dissimilar conclusions regarding a person's quality of life when the models are translated into forms of assessment. For example, opinions differ with regard to whether objective indicators of life conditions and life satisfaction are each components of quality of life, or whether only one of these represents quality of life (Borthwick-Duffy, 1992). Depending on the perspective of the evaluator, measurement will be based on either one or both constructs.

Evaluation usually leads to some kind of quantification; however, despite noteworthy efforts to address Landesman's invitation to conceptualize and operationally define quality of life, the fact remains that it is essentially a subjective construct that resists numerical scoring (Dennis, Williams, Giangreco, & Cloninger, 1993; Edgerton, 1990; Heinlein, 1994). As with the rapid development of measures of adaptive behavior in the 1970s (Meyers, Zetlin, & Nihira, 1979), numerous quality of life surveys have been produced in the past decade. It is easy to be critical of these instruments because, to a large extent, quality of life is in the eye of the beholder. Persons other than the survey authors are certain to take issue with the specific domains (i.e., the conceptual model) and measured indicators (operationalization of the model) contained on any survey. The researchers and practitioners who have either developed or utilized these instruments are not so naive as to think they have "solved" the dilemma of subjectivity, and that these measures capture the totality of an individual's life conditions and overall life satisfaction. While some writers have cautioned against reliance on instruments that are thought to oversimplify complex qualitative concepts like quality of life (Edgerton,

1990), and have even cautioned against the use of the quality of life term altogether (Luckasson, 1990), others have encouraged the use of multiple sources of information and data collection methodologies as a feasible approach to addressing this problem (Dennis et al., 1993; Heal & Sigelman, 1990; Lord & Pedlar, 1991). The following sections address issues that influence the way quality of life is conceptualized and subsequently measured.

Issues Influencing Conceptualization and Measurement

Considering subjective vs. objective indicators. Although most people agree that quality of life is primarily a subjective concept, it is not uncommon to find objective indicators in measurement protocols. Many writers have reviewed the literature that distinguishes between objective and subjective indicators of quality of life. Halpern (1993) described objective perspectives as reflecting society's point of view in the context of societal norms. In contrast, subjective perspectives represent an individual's point of view and are idiosyncratic. Some authors contend that when there is a lack of congruence between objective and subjective indicators, only the subjective indicators are valid descriptors of quality of life (Edgerton, 1990, Taylor & Bogdan, 1990). Others (e.g., Halpern, 1993; Heal, Borthwick-Duffy, & Saunders, in press; Rosen, 1986) note that one's perspective on individual choice, universal entitlements, personal needs, societal expectations, and social policy will influence the way quality of life is conceptualized, and thus, how it will be evaluated. It should be noted that objective quality of life indicators can be obtained through both qualitative and quantitative data methods; similarly, subjective information is also gathered through a variety of approaches, including quantitative, qualitative, and ecological methods (Dennis et al., 1993). If only subjective, only objective, or a combination of these indicators is used in the evaluation process, judgments regarding an individual's quality of life are likely to differ accordingly.

Empowerment and choice: By whose definition? The importance of empowerment and choice has been emphasized in the quality of life literature. Aspects of choice and decision-making are commonly found in quality of life assessment instruments. Goode (1990) defined a high quality of life as occurring when an individual's basic needs are met and he or she has the opportunity to pursue and achieve personal goals in major life settings, "while also satisfying the normative expectations that others hold for him or her in those settings" (p. 487). Halpern (1993) also described a tension that can exist between a person's choices and presumed societal norms, suggesting that sometimes a person's choices are in conflict with what society believes is in the best interest of individuals with disabilities. On the one hand, service systems advocate choice. On the other hand, we are sometimes critical when people with mental retardation make choices that we believe will lower the quality of their lives. For example, if a person prefers to do things that are not "age-appropriate," prefers to socialize in segregated activities, or enjoys outings with people who are paid to provide services to him, some conceptualizations and evaluative measures would rate his quality of life as being lower than if he engaged in activities that were less preferred by the individual but more consistent with societal norms or the principle of normalization. Sands and Kozleski (1994) also suggest that agencies sometimes act as a "buffer" between

individuals and societal norms, "engineering situations in which little individual choice is permitted" (p. 100), by restricting their ability to make those choices. If quality of life is to reflect what makes a person most satisfied or happy, how shall we evaluate choice and empowerment?

Evaluating goodness-of-fit. Quality of life is sometimes described as the goodness-of-fit of a person's needs and desires and the satisfaction of those needs (Dennis et al., 1993; Schalock, 1990; Schalock & Jensen, 1986). Ecological analyses have been proposed to measure the goodness-of-fit between a person's environment, resources, and stressors. Heal et al. (in press) further define quality of life as the discrepancy between needs and their fulfillment *through one's own control over the resources* (which can include various kinds of supports) to satisfy those needs. According to Heal et al., evaluation in terms of this definition requires a tool to compare objectively the disparity or discrepancy between an individual's needs and the degree and frequency with which they are met. Moreover, it requires an assessment of the extent to which supports are appropriate, i.e., whether they offer the most minimal assistance necessary, permit partial participation, or offer supported routines.

Quality of Life: A Single Definition and Method of Measurement?

The question of whether quality of life should be defined, evaluated, or interpreted according to the characteristics of the individual or of relatively homogeneous groups has not been fully answered. Goode (1990) and Schalock and Keith (1993) contend that quality of life for persons with disabilities comprises the same factors and relationships that are important to persons without disabilities. However, Flanagan (1982), who conducted a large-scale empirical investigation of quality of life measurement, suggested that some adjustments may have to be made to the dimensional structure of quality of life for persons with various disabilities. He further asserted that the specific questions used to measure the dimensions might have to be modified to take into account the limits imposed by disabilities. Along the same lines, Stade (1993) indicated that people with similar types of disabilities were in the best position to understand the impact of those particular disabilities on their quality of life. Parmenter (1988) noted, in relation to physical disabilities, that many persons must cope with the disability in addition to a lack of professional and economic resources. Moreover, disabilities reflect only part of what constitutes individual differences. It seems reasonable to propose that to be maximally useful, interpretation of quality of life evaluations must only be made for individuals or groups that have common characteristics, including severity and type of disability, gender, age, personality, interests and major life activities, and cultural background and environment. While there may be broad dimensions that describe quality of life and are common across most conceptual models, specific indicators of an individual's quality of life must extend beyond these general domains and consider specific characteristics of the individual. For example, when we identify empowerment and productivity as important dimensions of quality of life for all persons, or define quality of life in terms of goodness-of-fit, these are consistent with a universal conceptualization of quality of life. This common framework should not imply, though, that individuals with disabilities should accept lower quality of life standards simply because of the additional barriers they face. If requiring assistance or partial participation leads automatically to a lower quality of life score, this is what would happen. Neither does it contradict the belief that quality of life is "the same" for persons with and without disabilities. Rather, it emphasizes the need to consider individual differences, most of which are unrelated to the person's disability. It is important to know, for example, that an individual (with or without a disability) enjoys spending time alone. When this is the case and the person has infrequent social activity, his or her quality of life should not be considered worse than for someone who reports a greater frequency of social contacts or community involvement. The end result (overall life satisfaction, contentment, happiness, self-esteem) may be the same, but depending on individual differences, routes to that end are expected to differ.

Adults with and without disabilities: Use similar criteria? Sands and Kozleski (1994) based their comparative study on the assumption that quality of life should be the same for persons with and without disabilities, and that an accurate perspective depends on a "yardstick based on the typical patterns of adults in our communities" (p. 100). The majority (61%) of subjects with disabilities in their study had mental retardation. Original and modified versions of the Consumer Satisfaction Survey (Temple University, 1988) were used for group comparisons of persons with and without disabilities. This investigation assumed that services provided to persons with disabilities could be considered socially valid if the quality of life of those persons matched that of their typical peers. The study group of adults living in small community-based residences theoretically had access to the same activities and routines as the comparison group of persons without disabilities. They did not find a significant difference between the existence of a disability and overall satisfaction with life. Although the subjects with disabilities were generally satisfied with their lives, they rated themselves moderate to low in independence, a characteristic they considered important. The investigators explained this by suggesting overall satisfaction with life and quality of life (defined by specific measured components of life satisfaction) may not always be equivalent.

In the Sands and Kozleski (1994) study, efforts were made to produce comparable groups. One group, however, was identified because of their disabilities and differed from the other group in terms of marital history, income, and home ownership. The positive perceptions of quality of life of the group with disabilities, in spite of reported difficulties with transportation and their recognition of relatively lower levels of independence, suggest these individuals may have evaluated their overall quality of life in relation to other persons with disabilities, or that they were simply making intra-individual judgments about their own needs and achievements in the presence of their disabilities.

Considering level of disability.

Should quality of life be measured differently for persons with different degrees of disability? Should quality of life comparisons be made only within homogeneous groups? Finally, is it right to assume that if service systems are providing appropriate services and supports, that quality of life should be considered no differently than for persons without disabilities or for persons with different degrees of mental retardation? Responses to these questions can affect the way quality of life is operationalized, scored, and interpreted. Rosen (1986) raised the question of whether certain cognitive and social limitations of persons with mental retardation preclude certain types of advantages or options and also mandate certain needs not required

by persons without disabilities. If the above were found to be true, Rosen suggested, quality of life would need to be defined differently for people with mental retardation who were functioning at different levels of severity because it would be set on the basis of what could be "appreciated, responded to, integrated, and utilized by that individual" (p. 365). In the group studied by Sands and Kozleski (1994), care was taken to control for general levels of ability so both groups would have access to similar opportunities, and quality of life indicators would be expected to be similar. By controlling for these factors in their design, the investigators did not have to address the issues described above.

Significant correlations of quality of life scores with measures of IQ in the standardization sample of the Quality of Life Questionnaire (Schalock & Keith, 1993) lend support to the position that comparisons of quality of life should be made within relatively homogeneous groups of mental ability. Moreover, the psychometric properties of quantitative scales should be examined for different subgroups of people, especially those with varying degrees and types of adaptive competence. For example, although a small proportion of the Schalock et al. (1990) standardization sample had severe forms of retardation, the larger proportion of that sample and primary target group of the scale applications has been persons with relatively mild forms of retardation. Additional psychometric work focusing on samples with more severe disabilities is currently needed.

The relevance of severity or type of disability to an evaluation of quality of life can be examined from two perspectives. First, the ability to communicate can affect measurement. Cirrin and Rowland (1985) found in a sample of persons with severe communications deficits that they were capable of intentionally communicating through nonverbal means, and that great diversity existed in the types and frequency of communication styles used. Still, Heal and Sigelman (1990, 1992) report problems of acquiescence and of the inability to provide accurate judgments of aspects of quality of life among persons with limited mental ability. For individuals who are nonverbal, quality of life measures are typically completed by informants who know them well. The Quality of Life Questionnaire (Schalock & Keith, 1993), for example, can be completed by two persons who know the individual, and their scores averaged. For objective items this does not pose a problem. For indicators of satisfaction or other more subjective areas this could be problematic.

A second quality of life consideration for persons with varying degrees of retardation is the appropriateness of the measured variables, or at least the importance of comparing "peers" on quantified data. For a person who is medically fragile and is unable to move about, even with assistance, and is unresponsive to external stimulation, such indicators as citizenship or productivity in employment are probably less relevant to quality of life than other criteria, such as affective aspects of the environment and environmental stimulation. Even if the measured indicators of quality of life show variability among persons with different degrees of disability, unless what is measured represents the most meaningful indicators *for a particular group,* then the score that is produced has inadequate validity.

Different indicators across the life span? The quality of life for infants, children, adolescents, young adults, and elderly persons with or without mental retardation might be conceptualized in terms of similar overall constructs.

However, each stage of the life span brings unique considerations that may affect specific measured indicators. For example, children report school-related quality of life indicators, while adults of working age should respond to different questions about employment-related issues. Aging persons with developmental disabilities present new quality of life considerations compared to former generations, including increased longevity or Alzheimer's disease. Brown (1989) reported that systems concerned with elderly persons should be designed to maximize control and action of their clients, not overlooking the possible importance (and adaptability) of aggressive behavior in stabilizing and affecting life-style. Brown's (1989) recommendation that disability and aging should not be associated with external denial of initiative and risk-taking highlights potential differences in the ways quality of life should be measured and interpreted across the life span. The recommendations to consider the importance and validity of specific measured indicators for persons with different levels of disabilities are repeated here with regard to age. For example, because some items on the Quality of Life Questionnaire are not meaningful for younger people or do not constitute high priority domains, a student version of that instrument has been developed for school-age individuals (Keith & Schalock, 1995).

Behavior and emotional problems: Unique quality of life indicators?
Brown (1990) examined quality of life in terms of persons who have mental retardation and who also show symptoms of behavioral or emotional disturbance. He argued that our current focus on quality of life presents new opportunities to consider the particular case of these individuals who may be ignored or rejected by traditional psychiatric ser-

vices, and whose families may be unable to obtain appropriate services. Moreover, he cites evidence that emotional problems are not consistently recognized by those who work or live with individuals who have them. Because emotional problems may elicit varying responses from people who have different levels of tolerance, the reduction of inappropriate behavior in different contexts may lead to specific indicators of quality of life that are uniquely important to this group. This is another area in which the appropriateness of evaluation criteria and survey items should be carefully examined.

Considering other characteristics. The Canadian *Quality of Life Interview Schedule* (QUOLIS) is a system of assessment that reflects recent emphasis on the provision and degree of contentment with supports, along with individual choice. This assessment also considers the individual's personal characteristics, including secondary handicaps, energy level, sociability, reactivity to stress, and recent life events in the interpretation of quality of life data. Gender differences do not suggest the need for different measurement strategies or measured variables, but gender should be considered in the interpretation of quantitative and qualitative data, particularly during periods of puberty and menopause that differentially affect males and females (Quellette-Kuntz, 1990). In his study of postschool transition, Halpern (1993) found that gender was predictive of both personal fulfillment and vocational adjustment (i.e., being female was associated with lower outcome scores). Consistent with Goode's (1990) observation that quality of life must be understood within cultural contexts, Halpern (1993) also recommended that future research consider the cross-cultural validity of quality of life measures.

Measurement May Depend on the Purpose of Quality of Life Evaluation

As noted previously, the results of quality of life evaluations are used for a variety of purposes. At the individual level, a person's perceived quality of life can be monitored over time to examine the effects of contextual or other changes that are presumed to influence outcomes. With regard to program evaluation, Sands and Kozleski (1994) stressed the importance of evaluating the impact of services on outcomes and quality of life, rather than simply focusing on the successful delivery of services. In their view, interventions are only considered to be socially valid when their outcomes positively affect the quality of life of individuals participating in them. Quality of life evaluations are often domain-specific, focusing on a single area such as transition, employment, or residential placement. Not surprisingly, measurement can be affected by the overall goal of the evaluation, by the specific foci noted above, and by the unit of measurement (individuals, subgroups of people, programs, or agencies). In the sections below, quality of life definition and measurement are discussed in relation to specific domains or applications.

Special education transition programs. Halpern (1993) suggested that the concept of quality of life provides a useful framework for responding to federal special education mandates to define multidimensional transition outcomes and to develop measurement, research, and evaluation strategies that can document the attainment of these outcomes. This focus is relatively narrow when viewed in terms of a person's overall quality of life. When these objectives are met, individual-level data can be used to assist in individualized planning,

113

to monitor outcomes of transition goals on the Individualized Transition Plan (ITP), and to modify interventions when necessary to achieve successful outcomes. Aggregate data can be used to help agencies and organizations evaluate the effectiveness of transition programs in schools (Halpern, 1993).

Employment outcomes. Traditionally, objective indicators were used to evaluate employment outcomes in quality of life models. Halpern, Nave, Close, and Nelson (1986), for example, used employment status, job integration with persons without disabilities, and income after housing cost to define operationally an occupation factor in their community adjustment model. Interestingly, their occupational quality of life domain had low correlations ($r <$ .15) with the other quality of life components in their model, including general life satisfaction. From these findings it is difficult to know whether the low correlation is related to the objective vs. subjective indicator issue, or to the multidimensional nature of the quality of life construct. For example, a person might be generally satisfied with life while being unhappy in his or her job. Nevertheless, it serves to illustrate measurement issues that have been discussed in earlier sections.

Quality of life in competitive vs. sheltered employment. The comparative benefits of competitive job placements over sheltered workshops were studied by Inge, Banks, Wehman, Hill, and Shafer (1988). They considered adaptive skill acquisition and quality of life, defined as performance in domestic, community, leisure, vocational, and financial domains, as the relevant quality of life indicators. Although persons in competitive employment displayed higher skills in some domains of adaptive skills, the results did not support the hypothesis of a direct relationship

between skill acquisition and a positive change in the components of quality of life measured. This was consistent with Fabian (1991), who also reported that the empirical rehabilitation literature did not link higher levels of functioning with well-being, but would be inconsistent with the view that adaptive skills and quality of life have a direct, positive relationship.

A distinction between adaptive competency and quality of life was made by Baroff (1986), who indicated that adaptive competency should not be equated with happiness or personal life satisfaction. Should life satisfaction and "contentment" determine policies and define quality of life? Baroff also reminds us that if basic needs are being met, there will be no frustration or unhappiness and individuals are likely to report happiness and contentment. He states,

> *Because contentment is presumed possible in environments that are either protection- or growth-oriented, the adoption of a contentment or personal life satisfaction criterion is not without risks. It can be used to justify custodial rather than developmental services; it offers too much leeway to policy makers. It is more prudent to stress competency as a habilitative goal, while acknowledging that personal happiness cannot be ignored in the choices that we are allowed to make.*
>
> **(p. 367)**

A comparison of quality of life of workers in supported employment and sheltered workshops was conducted by Sinnott-Oswald, Gliner, and Spencer (1991), who used data based on the widely-used Quality of Life Questionnaire (Schalock & Keith, 1993) to obtain both objective and subjective quality of life information. In this study, "baseline" quality of life data was obtained by also sampling adults without disabilities. The authors contended that employment comparisons should consider more than numbers of workers placed, wages earned, and economic costs and benefits of different employment options. The study design and surveys addressed the hypothesis that more integrated employment experiences would lead to more environmental control, more community involvement, and positive perceptions of personal change. Item analyses showed greater frequencies of leisure and other activities, more mobility, higher self-esteem and job skill perceptions of workers in supported employment than among those in sheltered workshops. But there were also areas where differences were not found, especially in the environmental control domain (e.g., recreational activity selection, dining activity, shopping skills, living status). Samples were small in this study and comparability between groups was based only on age, gender, and general level of mental retardation. However, it is a good example of recent efforts to extend evaluations of community employment options beyond the traditional objective indicators that have been frequently used.

Relating employment outcomes to quality of life in other domains.

Schalock and Genung (1993) used personal interview, survey, and observational data to evaluate the current status, quality of life, and movement patterns of 85 individuals who had been placed into independent living and competitive employment 15 years earlier. Among other data collected, the Community Outcomes Scale (Schalock & Kiernan, 1990), the Quality of Life Questionnaire (Schalock & Keith, 1993), the Personal Satisfaction Survey (Schalock & Kiernan, 1990), and reported activity patterns were used to measure quality of life. The data were primarily analyzed in terms of two groups: those who were no longer receiving services of any kind (59%), and those who continued receiving services (19%). No differences were found between groups on two measures of satisfaction, community integration and how their time was used during non-work hours. As expected, the group not receiving services had better outcomes, including more productivity, independence, and control over decisions in their lives.

Residential placement.

Quality of life indices have been used to draw conclusions about residential placement policies and assumptions about least restrictive environments. Crapps, Langone, and Swaim (1985) utilized quality of life measurement in the evaluation of community-based group home placement. This study focused on two aspects of quality of life which have been hypothesized to be more predominant in smaller community-based residences than larger congregate facilities: active participation in integration activities and choice of activities (environmental control). Following extensive observation and direct interviews, they concluded that placement in group homes by itself did not seem to contribute to an overall increase in quality of life. The scope of quality of life was rather narrow in this study; however, it was sufficient to meet the study's objective.

The Lord and Pedlar (1991) follow-up study of an institution closure in British Columbia demonstrated an ecological approach to quality of life measurement. They conducted observations and interviewed the families and support staff of former residents who had multiple handicaps and were nonverbal. Based on the findings of the qualitative evaluation, they developed a self-administered questionnaire for group home managers. The survey responses confirmed the themes found in the observations and interviews: (1) little attention was given to the compatibility of people who were placed together after the closure; (2) some community settings seemed to be institutional-like, with few real opportunities for making important choices and with programming focused on simply keeping people active; and (3) even though the study participants were living in the community, they were not judged to be "of the community," lacking true relationships with people other than their paid staff. These recent findings echo those of Bjaanes and Butler (1974) during the peak of the deinstitutionalization movement, who also distinguished between physical integration and social, personal, or societal integration and found "institutional practices" in some group homes.

Quality of service and quality of life: Do they go hand in hand? In recent years service agencies have been expected to coordinate or provide services that lead to positive changes in the quality of life of their consumers. Fiscal accountability, parental and consumer satisfaction, and accreditation standards provide measures of the quality of care provided. Heinlein (1994) noted that the best measures of quality of care do not assure a high quality of life among the persons served. Further, the responsibility of state agencies is to establish parameters for quality of care that allow service providers the flexibility to address quality of life. Finally, he suggests that "the gap between quality of care at the macro level and quality of life at the

micro level cannot be spanned by a system that focuses on only one level" (p. 375).

Future Directions

It would be naive to think that mental retardation professionals will ever agree on a universal conceptualization of quality of life. This chapter has reviewed some of the philosophical differences that would prevent a concensus. Those who firmly believe that quality of life is determined only by subjective assessments from the individual, for example, are unlikely to embrace a definition that also includes objective indices of life conditions. Likewise, the question of whether or not the same indicators should characterize quality of life for all people, regardless of handicap, personal preferences, or other characteristics, also draws varied but firm responses from those concerned with evaluating this construct. Neither researchers, service providers, nor administrators are likely to reconstruct their perspectives on these and other issues in the interest of developing a single definition of quality of life. Therefore, if definition must precede evaluation, and if a widely accepted definition is required, then quality of life measurement will be in an indefinite holding pattern.

For those involved in quality of life evaluation, the methods of measurement they select will most likely reflect their assumptions about qualitative and quantitative data, subjective and objective indicators, and the validity of self-report and ecological approaches to obtaining information. Perspectives on these measurement issues, combined with differences in conceptualization, can lead to varied conclusions about the quality of life of a given individual, program, or group. Studies that seek to identify predictors or correlates of a good quality of life can also produce different findings, depending on the definition and corresponding measurement approach that is used. Moreover, it is certainly possible that decisions that rely on this information are likely to lead to very different outcomes when the quality of life estimates are dissimilar.

During the decade that has passed since Landesman's (1986) guest editorial in *Mental Retardation,* considerable progress has been made. The scientific and professional community has been actively addressing definitional and measurement issues. While it is impor-tant to recognize that different perspectives on this abstract, subjective construct and different approaches to its measurement will affect the findings of any evaluation, the results can still lead to better informed decisions. A cautious approach to interpretation, along with continued efforts to identify common viewpoints and refine evaluation procedures, should ultimately lead to a better quality of life for individuals with mental retardation.

Author Note

This report was funded in part by grants HD22953 and HD21056 from the National Institute of Child Health and Human Development.

References

Baroff, G.S. (1986). Maximal adaptive competency. *Mental Retardation, 24,* 367-368.

Bjaanes, A.T., & Butler, E.W. (1974). Environmental variations in community care facilities for mentally retarded persons. *American Journal on Mental Retardation, 78,* 429-439.

Borthwick-Duffy, S.A. (1992). Quality of life and quality of care. In L. Rowitz (Ed.), *Mental retardation in the year 2000* (pp. 52-65). New York: Springer-Verlag.

Brown, R.I. (1989). Aging, disability and quality of life: A challenge for society. *Canadian Psychology, 30,* 551-559.

Brown, R.I. (1990). Quality of life for people with learning difficulties: The challenge for behavioural and emotional disturbance. *International Review of Psychiatry, 2,* 23-32.

Cirrin, F.M., & Rowland, C.M. (1985). Communicative assessment of nonverbal youths with severe/profound mental retardation. *Mental Retardation, 23,* 52-62.

Crapps, J.M., Langone, J., & Swaim, S. (1985). Quality and quantity of participation in community environments by mentally retarded adults. *Education and Training in Mental Retardation, 20,* 123-129.

Dennis, R.E., Williams, W., Giangreco, M.F., & Cloninger, C.J. (1993). Quality of life as context for planning and evaluating services. *Exceptional Children, 59,* 449-512.

Edgerton, R.B. (1990). Quality of life from a longitudinal research perspective. In R.L. Schalock (Ed.), *Quality of life: Perspectives and issues* (pp. 149-160). Washington, DC: American Association on Mental Retardation.

Fabian, E. (1991). Using quality of life indicators in rehabilitation program evaluation. *Rehabilitation Counseling Bulletin, 34,* 334-356.

Flanagan, J.C. (1982). Measurement of quality of life: Current state of the art. *Archives of Physical and Medical Rehabilitation, 63,* 56-69.

Goode, D. (1990). Thinking about and discussing quality of life. In R.L. Schalock (Ed.), *Quality of life: Perspectives and issues* (pp. 41-57). Washington, DC: American Association on Mental Retardation.

Halpern, A.S. (1993). Quality of life and a conceptual framework for evaluating transition outcomes. *Exceptional Children, 59,* 486-498.

Halpern, A., Nave, G., Close, D., & Nelson, D. (1986). An empirical analysis of the dimensions of community adjustment for adolescents and young adults with disabilities. *Australia and New Zealand Journal of Developmental Disabilities, 15,* 1-13.

Heal, L., & Sigelman, C. (1990). Methodological issues in measuring quality of life in individuals with mental retardation. In R.L. Schalock (Ed.), *Quality of life: Perspectives and issues* (pp. 161-176). Washington, DC: American Association on Mental Retardation.

Heal, L.W., & Sigelman, C.K. (1992, December). *Interviewing respondents who have limited mental ability.* Paper presented at the International Symposium on the Assessment of Exceptional Children, Changhua, Taiwan.

Heal, L.W., Borthwick-Duffy, S.A., & Saunders, R.R. (1995). Assessment of quality of life. In J.W. Jacobson & J.A. Mulick (Eds.), *Manual of diagnosis and professional practice in mental retardation.* Washington, DC: American Psychological Association.

Heinlein, K.B. (1994). Quality of care, quality of life: A rural perspective. *Mental Retardation, 32,* 374-376.

Inge, K.J., Banks, D., Wehman, P., Hill, J., & Shafer, M.S. (1988). Quality of life for individuals who are labeled mentally retarded. Evaluating competitive employment versus sheltered workshop employment. *Education and Training in Mental Retardation, 6,* 97-104.

Keith, K.D., & Schalock, R.L. (1995). *Student Quality of Life Questionnaire.* Worthington, OH: IDS.

Landesman, S. (1986). Quality of life and personal life satisfaction: Definition and measurement issues. *Mental Retardation, 24,* 141-143.

Lord, J., & Pedlar, A. (1991). Life in the community: Four years after the closure of an institution. *Mental Retardation, 29,* 213-221.

Luckasson, R. (1990). A lawyer's perspective on quality of life. In R.L. Schalock (Ed.), *Quality of life: Perspectives and issues* (pp. 211-214). Washington, DC: American Association on Mental Retardation.

Lusthaus, E.W. (1985). Involuntary euthanasia and current attempts to define persons with mental retardation as less than human. *Mental Retardation, 23,* 148-154.

Meyers, C.E., Zetlin, A., & Nihira, K. (1979). The measurement of adaptive behavior. In N.R. Ellis (Ed.), *Handbook of Mental Deficiency* (2nd ed., pp. 431-481). New York: Ehrlbaum.

Parmenter, T. (1988). An analysis of the dimensions of quality of life for people with physical disabilities. In R.I. Brown (Ed.), *Quality of life and handicapped people* (pp. 105-120). London: Croom Helm.

Powell, T.H., & Hecimovic, A. (1985). Baby Doe and the search for a quality life. *Exceptional Children, 51,* 315-323.

Quellette-Kuntz, H. (1990). A pilot study in the use of the *Quality of Life Interview Schedule. Social Indicators Research, 23,* 283-298.

Rosen, M. (1986). Quality of life for persons with mental retardation: A question of entitlement. *Mental Retardation, 24,* 365-366.

Sands, D.J., & Kozleski, E.B. (1994). Quality of life differences between adults with and without disabilities. *Education and Training in Mental Retardation and Developmental Disabilities, 29,* 90-101.

Schalock, R.L. (1990). Where do we go from here? In R.L. Schalock (Ed.), *Quality of life: Perspectives and issues* (pp. 235-240). Washington, DC: American Association on Mental Retardation.

Schalock, R.L., & Genung, L.T. (1993). Placement from a community-based mental retardation program: A 15-year follow-up. *American Journal on Mental Retardation, 98,* 400-407.

Schalock, R.L., & Jensen, C.M. (1986). Assessing the goodness-of-fit between persons and their environments. *Journal of the Association for Persons with Severe Handicaps, 11,* 103-109.

Schalock, R.L., & Keith, K.D. (1993). *Quality of life questionnaire.* Worthington, OH: IDS.

Schalock, R.L., & Kiernan, K.D. (1990). *Habilitation planning for adults with disabilities.* New York: Springer-Verlag.

Sinnott-Oswald, M., Gliner, J.A., & Spencer, K.C. (1991). Supported and sheltered employment: Quality of life issues among workers with disabilities. *Education and Training in Mental Retardation and Developmental Disabilities, 24,* 388-397.

Stade, N.K. (1993). The use of quality-of-life measures to ration health care: Reviving a rejected proposal. *Columbia Law Review, 93,* 1985-2021.

Taylor, S., & Bogdan, R. (1990). Quality of life and the individual's perspective. In R.L. Schalock (Ed.), *Quality of life: Perspectives and issues* (pp. 27-40). Washington, DC: American Association on Mental Retardation.

Temple University (1988). *A national survey of consumers of services with developmental disabilities.* Final survey instrument. Unpublished instrument. Washington, DC: National Developmental Disabilities Planning Council.

119

Part III

Conceptualization and Measurement of Quality of Life

As either a sensitizing concept or research construct, the concept of quality of life has definitely become an overarching issue in the field of mental retardation and developmental disabilities. In the book's final chapter, I attempt to synthesize the material presented in the preceding chapters that reflects significant advances in our understanding of this important concept. I also discuss key conceptual and measurement issues that still need to be resolved through ongoing discourse and research. These eight issues are phrased as questions to facilitate discussion and research:

1. How should we refer to the term, "quality of life?"

2. Is quality of life a single, unitary entity, or a multidimensional, interactive concept?

3. How is it best to conceptualize indicators of quality of life?

4. Is quality of life the same for all individuals?

5. What should be measured in reference to quality of life?

6. How do we measure quality of life?

7. What measurement standards need to be considered?

8. How do we overcome measurement challenges?

In the Preface, I pointed out that quality of life is not a new concept, and indeed, people since antiquity have pursued the dimensions of a life of quality. What is different today— and what makes the concept so important to our field—is our attempt to use the concept as a process and an overriding principle to improve the lives of persons with mental retardation and closely related disabilities, and to evaluate the social validity of current (re)habilitation efforts.

Public policy and (re)habilitation organizations are struggling to reformulate themselves within a quality of life paradigm reflective of the current quality revolution. They need the most current thinking about the concept of quality of life and its measurement, so that they can enhance service quality and further develop quality of life as a construct that is applicable to society as a whole. Because people with disabilities are vulnerable to shifting social, political, and economic trends, the concept of quality of life provides a fundamentally positive and growth-oriented principle that can be the basis for developing a national and international policy towards people with disabilities. Why? Because it steers us in the right direction: towards self-determination, person-centered planning, supporting people's needs and desires, and asking people what they think and how they feel.

But we still have work to do. Thus, throughout this final chapter, I challenge the reader to consider and respond to the following five heuristic arguments:

1. Quality of life for persons with disabilities is composed of those same factors and relationships that are important to all persons.

2. Quality of life should be viewed as an organizing concept—not an entity—that can be used for multiple purposes.

3. There is a consensual set of core quality of life dimensions and associated measurable indicators.

4. Quality of life measurement should encompass a multimethodological perspective and use psychometrically sound measurement standards.

5. Quality of life is a fundamental principle and process that is applicable to society as a whole, and thus provides a valuable reference and guide for (re)habilitation services and their evaluation.

Reconsidering the Conceptualization and Measurement of Quality of Life

Robert L. Schalock
Hastings College

Why are the conceptualization and measurement of quality of life so important? From my perspective, the importance of these issues stems from at least three sources. First, the concept of quality of life is emerging as an overarching principle that is applicable to the betterment of society as a whole in this time of social, political, technological, and economic transformations. Second, the current paradigm shift in mental retardation and closely related disabilities, with its emphasis on self-determination, inclusion, equity, empowerment, community-based supports, and quality outcomes has forced service providers to focus on an enhanced quality of life for persons with disabilities. And third, the quality revolution, with its emphasis on total quality, quality leadership, and total quality management, has resulted in a movement within human services toward managing for quality. Nevertheless, a concensus has not been reached about the definition or conceptual framework for quality of life.

In this chapter's four major sections I attempt to synthesize the material presented in the preceding chapters. These four sections cover the conceptualization of quality of life, the measurement of quality of life, conceptual and measurement issues, and quality of life as an organizing concept. Throughout the chapter I will argue the following:

- The conceptualization of quality of life includes core principles and dimensions.

- Instead of an entity that one has or does not have to some degree, quality of life should be viewed as an organizing concept.

- As an organizing concept, quality of life can be used for a number of purposes, including evaluating consensual core dimensions associated with a life of quality; providing direction and guidance in providing appropriate services; and using the resulting data for multiple purposes.

- We need to move away from viewing quality of life as composed of various subjective and objective indicators to the realization that there are a consensual set of core quality of life dimensions and associated indicators that can be measured from a multimethodological perspective, depending upon the investigator's purpose.

- The multidimensional perspective includes three measurement techniques: participant observation, performance-based assessment, and standardized instruments.

The Conceptualization of Quality of Life

Core Quality of Life Principles

In the first section of this volume quality of life was discussed as a sensitizing concept with several key characteristics:

- It is best understood from the perspective of the individual, which requires in-depth knowledge of the person.

- It embodies general feelings of well-being, opportunities to fulfill one's hopes and dreams, and positive social interactions.

- It cannot be separated from an individual's developmental stage, supports network, and relevant life domains.

- It gives us a sense of reference and guidance in approaching quality of life issues.

In addition to the above conceptualization issues, a number of core quality of life principles were also identified. These core principles can serve as a basis for both a further conceptualization of the concept of quality of life and the measurement and use of quality of life data. Eight core quality of life principles are summarized in Table 12.1. Throughout the table note the importance of concepts such as self-determination, equity, opportunities, empowerment, inclusion, knowing the person, and the multidimensionality of one's life.

Core Quality of Life Dimensions

One of the most exciting changes in recent years has been the emerging consensus of what constitutes the core dimensions of a life of quality. Interest in these dimensions goes back to the pioneering work of Thorndike in the 1930s (Thorndike, 1939). Historically, the social scientists' attempts to conceptualize the core dimensions of quality of life fall into the following three perspectives (Schalock, 1990): social indicators, psychological indicators, and goodness-of-fit/social policy.

1. *Social indicators* generally refer to external, environmentally-based conditions such as health, social welfare, friendships, standard of living, education, public safety, housing, neighborhood, and leisure. These indicators may be defined as a statistic of direct normative interest that facilitates concise, comprehensive, and balanced judgments about the conditions of major aspects of either society or one's life (Andrews & Whithey, 1976).

2. *Psychological indicators* focus on a person's subjective reactions to life experiences and are usually measured from one of two perspectives:

Table 12.1
Core Quality of Life Principles

1. Quality of life for persons with disabilities is composed of those same factors and relationships that are important to all persons.

2. Quality of life is experienced when a person's basic needs are met and when he or she has the same opportunities as anyone else to pursue and achieve goals in the major life settings of home, community, school, and work.

3. Quality of life is a multidimensional concept that can be consensually validated by a wide range of persons representing a variety of viewpoints of consumers and their families, advocates, professionals, and providers.

4. Quality of life is enhanced by empowering persons to participate in decisions that affect their lives.

5. Quality of life is enhanced by the acceptance and full integration of persons into their local communities.

6. Quality of life is an organizing concept that can be used for a number of purposes including evaluating those core dimensions associated with a life of quality, providing direction and reference in approaching customer services, and assessing persons' feelings of satisfaction and well-being.

7. The study of quality of life requires an in-depth knowledge of people and their perspectives and multiple methodologies.

8. The measurement of quality of life requires multiple measurement techniques.

psychological well-being or personal satisfaction. An example of the first perspective is the work of Flanagan (1982), who identified five general dimensions of quality of life: physical and material well-being; relations with other people; social, community, and civic activities; personal development and fulfillment; and recreation. The second perspective underlies the work of Heal and associates (Harner & Heal, 1993; Heal, Rubin, & Park, 1995), who measure the individual's satisfaction with factors such as home and community, friends, leisure activities, self-control and social support and safety.

3. *The goodness-of-fit/social policy* perspective proposes that quality of life is related to a match between a person's wants or needs and their fulfillment. For example, the goodness-of-fit model proposed by Murrell and Norris (1983) suggests that the characteristics of a given group interact with the resources and stressors of the environment, and that the quality of a person's life is a function of the discrepancy between the resources and the stressors. Similarly, Jamieson (1993) suggests that measurement of quality of life should focus on the degree of congruence between needs and their satisfied fulfillment. And finally, Saunders and Spradlin (1991) and Schalock and Jensen (1986) propose that quality of life measurement should consider the congruence between environmental demands and a person's control of resources or skills to meet these demands. In this regard, we have demonstrated (Schalock, Keith, Hoffman, & Karan, 1989) a positive relationship between measures of quality of life and the goodness-of-fit between a person

and his or her living and employment environments.

It is clear in this volume that one's quality of life includes a number of core dimensions and associated quality indicators. Eight core quality of life dimensions and associated indicators are summarized in Table 12.2. They are based on the material presented in this volume plus work by Campbell (1976); Campbell, Converse, and Rogers (1976); Chen (1988); Cummins (1995); Heal, Borthwick-Duffy, and Saunders (1995); Hughes, Hwang, Kim, Eisenman, and Killian (1995); Keith, Heal, and Schalock (in press); and The Accreditation Council (1993).

Note the experiential and empirical nature of each of the consensual core quality of life dimensions:

- Emotional well-being

- Interpersonal relationships

- Material well-being

- Personal development

- Physical well-being

- Self-determination

- Social inclusion

- Rights

The Measurement of Quality of Life

Significant conceptual breakthroughs resulting from material presented in this volume and other quality of life measurement research (Cf. Schalock, 1994, 1995) have resulted in the emerging consensus that each of the eight core quality of life dimensions summarized in Table 12.2 can be measured using a multimethod-ological perspective, depending upon the investigator's focus and purpose. I argue in this section that

there is no need to make the somewhat artificial distinction between objective and subjective indicators of quality of life. Rather, I suggest that one should use one or more of the indicators of the core dimension(s) of interest (see Table 12.2) and measure them through one (or more) of the three suggested measurement techniques: participant observation, performance-based assessment, or standardized instruments. These three techniques and a process model for completing the measurement are presented below.

Measurement Techniques

A basic point made repeatedly throughout this volume is that quality of life is a multidimensional construct. Thus, its measurement needs to use one or more methods, depending upon the investigator's focus and purpose. The use of multiple measurement techniques is based on a number of premises: (a) Quality of life is a multidimensional construct in which culturally consensual values and shared attitudes are reflected; (b) individuals differ in their ability to understand and respond; (3) people use quality of life data for different purposes including self-report, description, evaluation, and comparison; and (4) the utilization of quality of life data can focus on either the individual or a group. It is within this context that the following three measurement techniques are discussed.

1. *Participant observation* requires that data collectors observe what people do, listen to what they say, and frequently participate in their daily activities to get a better sense of their lives. This technique also lends itself nicely to attitude surveys regarding life satisfaction, consumer satisfaction, feelings of well-being, and person-environmental interactions. The investigator can also study

Table 12.2
Core Quality of Life Dimensions and Indicators

Dimension	Exemplary Indicators
1. Emotional Well-Being	Safety Spirituality Happiness Freedom from Stress Self-Concept Contentment
2. Interpersonal Relations	Intimacy Affection Family Interactions Friendships Supports
3. Material Well-Being	Ownership Financial Security Food Employment Possessions Social Economic Status Shelter
4. Personal Development	Education Skills Fulfillment Personal Competence Purposeful Activity Advancement
5. Physical Well-Being	Health Nutrition Recreation Mobility Health Care Health Insurance Leisure Activities of Daily Living
6. Self-Determination	Autonomy Choices Decisions Personal Control Self-Direction Personal Goals/Values
7. Social Inclusion	Acceptance Status Supports Work Environment Community Integration and Participation Roles Volunteer Activities Residential Environment
8. Rights	Privacy Voting Access Due Process Ownership Civic Responsibilities

the behavior and interactions displayed in natural settings in order to describe in detail the person's life.

> *Our ethnographic procedures required familiarity with as many aspects of a person's life as possible. Our methodological philosophy derives primarily from naturalism, rather than positive behavioral science. We attempt to comprehend and interpret the phenomena under study as faithfully as possible; our goal is to be true to the phenomena themselves...To carry out ethnographic naturalism, we must have prolonged contact with people. We must become, if only relatively so, a natural part of their lives.*
>
> **(Edgerton, 1990, p. 154)**

2. *Performance-based assessment* is defined as using objective indicators to evaluate a person's core quality of life dimensions. Table 12.2 listed a number of indicators that can be used in such assessment. For example, if one is interested in evaluating physical well-being, objective indicators such as health status, health care coverage, nutritional status, or recreation and leisure activities could be used. On the other hand, one could use these same indicators to ask how the person feels about them or how satisfied the person is with them. If this is done, one is then using a participant observation technique. Thus, the same quality of life indicator(s) can be used to evaluate

127

either the subjective or objective aspect of the core quality of life dimension. What is different is the measurement technique used.

3. *Standardized instruments* are used frequently to assess a number of indicators reflective of life quality. Table 12.3 lists a number of published standardized instruments with a summary of the quality of life dimensions or indicators that each assesses. This listing indicates that the most common factors assessed by current quality of life instruments include home and community living, financial employment, possessions, social integration (family, friends, natural supports), health status and safety, personal control, choices, and decision-making. These factors lend empirical support to the core consensual quality of life dimensions summarized in Table 12.2.

Measurement Standards

Himmel (1984) suggests three criteria for choosing a measurement technique: psychometric quality, a graded response format, and utility. To those, I would add three essential measurement standards that apply to each of the three measurement techniques just discussed: reliability, validity, and standardization group.

1. *Reliability* refers to the consistency of one's measures. The most common types of reliability include test-retest, inter/intraobserver, and internal consistency. Reliability coefficients should generally be within the .80 to .85 range for the technique to be reliable.

2. *Validity* refers to whether one's technique is measuring what it purports to measure. Common forms of validity include content (Do the measurement items measure

Table 12.3
Quality of Life Assessment Instruments for Persons with Disabilities

Author (Instruments)	Quality of Life Dimension/Indicator(s)
Brown, Bayer, and MacFarlane (1989) (QOL Questionnaire)	Income Health Life Satisfaction Environment Growth and Mastery Skills Psychological Well-Being Perception of Skills and Needs
Cummins et al. (1994) (Comprehensive QOL Scale)	Safety Health Intimacy Material Things Productivity Emotional Well-Being Place in Society
Evans, Burns, Robinson, and Garrett (1985) (QOL Questionnaire)	Well-Being in Areas of Social Family Physical Occupational Personal Material
Heal, Rubin, and Park (1995) (Satisfaction Interview Scale)	Friends Self Control Employment Home and Community Leisure Activities
Halpern, Nave, Close, and Nelson (1986) (Test Battery)	Occupation Residential Environment Client Satisfaction Social Support/Safety
Harner and Heal (1993) (Multifaceted Lifestyle Satisfaction Scale)	Friends Self Control Employment Home and Community Leisure Activies
Keith and Schalock (1995) (Quality of Student Life Questionnaire)	Well-being Social Satisfaction Empowerment/Control Belonging
Schalock and Keith (1993) (Quality of Life Questionnaire)	Satisfaction Productivity Independence/ Decision Making Community Integration

what the test/method intends to measure?), construct (Do the items measure the underlying construct being investigated?), predictive (Do the person's test results actually predict future performance or satisfaction?), and concurrent (Are the current results consistent with a second, independent measure of the indicator or dimension?) Validity coefficients should generally be within at least the .60 to .70 range for the measure to be considered valid.

3. *Standardization group.* If quality of life data are used for evaluation or comparison purposes, then one needs to ask: On whom was the measure developed and standardized for comparative purposes? One needs to be very careful not to use norms for comparisons that were not developed on individuals similar to those on whom the measurement was made. This is an essential standard for subgroup comparisons and in today's multicultural and consumer-oriented worlds.

Measurement Process

There are three aspects to measuring quality of life dimensions and core indicators that one needs to consider. First, what measurement technique should one use in reference to assessing the various core dimensions/indicators? Second, how does one interface the three measurement techniques discussed above with one or more uses of quality of life data? And third, what sequential process does one employ to ensure reliable and valid information? Each of these aspects is considered below.

1. *Framework for measuring core quality of life dimensions.* A framework for using one or more measurement techniques is outlined in Table 12.4. The table is built around the three measurement techniques discussed previously and the eight core quality of life dimensions listed in Table 12.2. Note three aspects to the matrix. First, the core quality of life dimensions are listed down the side. Second, one can use any one of three measurement techniques:

Table 12.4
A Framework for Measuring Core Quality of Life Dimensions

Core Dimension	Measurement Technique		
	Participant Observation	Performance Based Assessment	Standardized Instruments
Emotional Well-Being	X		X
Interpersonal Relations	X		
Material Well-Being	X	X	
Personal Development	X	X	X
Physical Well-Being	X	X	X
Self-Determination	X	X	
Social Inclusion	X	X	X
Rights	X	X	

participant observation, performance-based assessment, or standardized instruments. And third, the "x" denotes the suggested technique to use to measure the core dimension.

2. *Interfacing measurement techniques with data use.* In Volume II we will discuss the multiple uses of quality of life data. For our purposes here, it is sufficient to recognize that there are at least eight major uses: assessing satisfaction levels; determining feelings of general well-being; assessing persons' needs; assessing (re)habilitation program outcomes; providing formative feedback to various stakeholders; informing program development or change, policy development, and the conduct of research. A matrix that shows the relationship between the three measurement techniques and each of these data uses is presented in Table 12.5. The matrix is organized in the same way as Table 12.4, with potential data uses listed along the side and the three measurement

techniques listed across the top. The "x" denotes the suggested technique for the respective data use.

3. *Sequential measurement process.* Once one has decided on the core quality of life dimension to measure, the intended use of the resulting data, and the specific measurement technique that will be used, then it is potentially beneficial to "walk through" a 6-step process that should insure reliable, valid, and useful data. This 6-step process is outlined in Figure 12.1 and includes the following specific steps.

Step 1. Determine the purpose of your investigation and the intended use of the data sets (see Table 12.5).

Step 2. Select the core quality of life dimension that will answer the data needs and fulfill the purpose of one's investigation (see Table 12.2).

Step 3. Select the core quality of life indicator(s) (see Table 12.2 for exemplary indicators).

Table 12.5
A Framework for Interfacing Measurement Techniques with Data Uses

Data Use	Measurement Technique		
	Participant Observation	Performance Based Assessment	Standardized Instruments
Satisfaction Level	X	X	X
Well-Being	X	X	X
Needs Assessment	X		
Outcomes Assessment		X	X
Formative Feedback	X	X	X
Program Development/Change	X	X	
Policy Development			X
Research	X	X	X

Figure 12.1
Quality of Life
Measurement Flowchart

STEP 1

**Determine Purpose of Investigation
and Intended Use of the Data**

Assess Satisfaction	Provide Formative Feedback
Assess Well-Being	Change Program
Assess Needs	Develop Policy
Assess Outcomes	Conduct Research

STEP 2

Select Core Quality of Life Dimension(s)

Emotional Well-Being	Physical Well-Being
Interpersonal Relations	Self-Determination
Material Well-Being	Social Inclusion
Personal Development	Rights

STEP 3

**Select Core Dimension Indicator(s)
(See Table 12.2)**

STEP 4

Select Measurement Technique(s)

Participant Observation
Performance-Based Assessment
Standardized Instrument

STEP 5

**Demonstrate Reliable and Valid
Measurement of Core Indicator(s)**

STEP 6

Interpret Results

Step 4. Select the measurement technique that will best provide the data that one needs. Keep in mind the issues of time, expertise, group composition, and demonstrated reliability and validity of the technique selected. The technique selected will depend upon both the core quality of life dimension one is interested in and the designated use of the quality of life data (see Tables 12.4 and 12.5).

Step 5. Demonstrate acceptable reliability and validity. In this regard, be sure not to overlook the following three issues: (a) what core dimension (or construct) is actually being measured; (b) is the construct/dimension being measured validly; and (c) is the construct/dimension being measured reliably?

Step 6. Interpret the results cautiously. As discussed in previous chapters, there are a number of potential problems and challenges in measuring these dimensions. Chief among them include weaknesses of the measures, problems with the task variables being assessed, response and acquiescent biases among respondents, and possible effects of the interview itself.

Conceptual and Measurement Issues

The above discussion of the conceptualization and measurement of quality of life points out a number of conceptual and measurement issues that still need to be resolved. Readers will undoubtedly agree that we have made significant progress in recent years in understanding and measuring the core dimensions of quality of life. But we still need to focus on some key conceptual and measurement issues, as discussed below.

Conceptual Issues

The concept of quality of life is a multifaceted construct. Throughout this volume it has been referred to as a sensitizing concept and a research construct. I have also suggested that it can serve as an organizing concept that provides direction and guidance in our work to improve life conditions of all persons. It is still apparent, however, that a clear conceptualization of quality of life is still emerging. My understanding of the literature suggests that four conceptual issues need to be resolved before a reasonable consensus can be reached. I have expressed each of these issues as a question to clarify the issue and stimulate our discourse.

1. **How should we refer to the term "quality of life?"**

2. **Is quality of life a single, unitary entity, or a multidimensional interactive concept?**

3. **How is it best to conceptualize indicators of quality of life?**

4. **Is quality of life the same for all individuals?**

1. **How should we refer to the term "quality of life?"** Currently, there are over 100 definitions and models of quality of life (Cummins, 1995). While Spitzer (1987) found only four articles with "quality of life in their titles" between 1968 and 1970, Hughes et al. (1995) reported 87 studies between 1972 and 1993 that met the research criterion. This rapid increase undoubtedly reflects both the tremendous interest in the concept of quality of life and the lack of consensus regarding its meaning. Thus, the question: Are we better off with a definition of quality of life, or would we be further ahead to consider quality of life as a working construct or organizing concept?

2. **Is quality of life a single or multidimensional construct?** The earlier work on quality of life implied that it is a single or unitary entity that could be expressed as global satisfaction, well-being, or happiness. Subsequently, the emphasis has shifted to considering quality of life as a multidimensional, interactive construct. For example, Hughes et al. (1995) suggests that environmental factors interact with personal demographic characteristics to influence a person's quality of life. Similarly, Heal, Borthwick-Duffy, & Saunders (1995) suggest that quality of life reflects global satisfaction with one's life-style and control over the human and environmental resources that produce satisfaction. Finally, Zautra and Goodhart (1979) suggest that

> *...quality of life pertains to the goodness of life that resides in the quality of life experience, both as subjectively evaluated and as objectively determined by an assessment of external conditions.*
>
> **(p. 1)**

3. **How is it best to conceptualize indicators?** Historically, as indicated in the quote from Zautra and Goodhart, a distinction has been made between the objective and subjective indicators of quality of life. Subjective indicators focused on

the individual's feelings of well-being and satisfaction; objective indicators focused on normative factors such as life-style, income, and objective conditions of living. The important conceptual issue to resolve is whether we are better off to continue this distinction, or does it make better sense (as argued in this chapter) to consider a number of potential indicators that can be assessed from either a subjective or objective perspective.

4. **Is quality of life the same for all individuals?** Initially, quality of life was referenced to the population at large and thus objective, normative comparison of quality of life indicators was logical (Andrews & Whitney, 1976; Campbell, 1976; Campbell et al., 1976). In the mid 1980s, the concept began to appear in the mental retardation/developmental disabilities literature. At the same time, Flanagan (1982) suggested that quality of life for persons with disabilities should be evaluated within the context of their condition. This notion was reinforced in the significant work of Borthwick-Duffy (1990), who suggested that

Certainly the evaluation and measurement of life quality must follow a clear delineation of the important dimensions of quality of life, keeping in mind that, regardless of intelligence level, individuals will differ in their preferences and their own perceptions of what constitutes a good quality of life.

(p. 186)

Others, however, have raised the question as to whether or not quality of life (as a concept) should be considered the same for all persons within a given language/cultural grouping. Goode (1990, 1994) and Schalock and Keith (1993) suggest that we should conceptualize quality of life similarly for persons with or without disabilities. This notion is consistent with the first core quality of life principle listed in Table 12.1. Similarly, Cummins (1995) states that

It is imperative that all definitions and models of quality of life be referenced to the general population both in their conception and operational measures.

(p. 14)

This fourth question is not insignificant. It may well be that we can agree on the fundamental dimensions (or outcomes) of a quality of life model that do not vary for individuals with or without disabilities, although the process for achieving these outcomes may be idiosyncratic to each person (Borthwick-Duffy, 1990; Hughes et al., 1995).

In answering this fourth question we should not overlook the real possibility of cultural differences in the conceptualization of quality of life, including its core dimensions and indicators. We still have considerable work to do in this area and are just beginning work in cross-cultural assessment (Keith, this volume; Keith, Yamamoto, Okita, & Schalock, 1995; Schalock et al., 1990). For example, we have recently reported (Keith, Heal, & Schalock, in press) reasonably good agreement across seven language groups on the value ascribed to 10 key quality of life concepts including rights, relationships, satisfaction, environment, economic

133

security and well-being, social inclusion, individual control, privacy, health, and growth and development.

Measurement Issues

Progress in the measurement of the quality of life construct during recent years is reflected in the general agreement found in the measurement literature about the core quality of life dimensions (Table 12.2) and the concordance among quality of life indicators assessed on current measurement instruments (Table 12.3). Despite this progress, my understanding of the quality of life measurement literature suggests that the following four measurement issues still need to be resolved.

1. **What should be measured?**

2. **How do we measure quality of life?**

3. **What psychometric standards need to be considered?**

4. **How do we overcome measurement challenges?**

1. **What should be measured?** We cannot completely answer this question until we have resolved the first two conceptual issues discussed in the previous section: How should we refer to the term quality of life, and is quality of life a single, unitary entity or a multidimensional, interactive construct? In the meantime, we need to discuss whether it is best to evaluate one or more of the core quality of life dimensions or indicators listed in Tables 12.2 and 12.3; should we continue to use unitary measures (such as global satisfaction, well-being, or happiness); or should we continue to make the distinction between subjective and objective indicators? A related issue is whether various dimensions of quality of life should be weighted differentially, as suggested in this volume by Felce and Perry (see Figure 7.1) and elsewhere by Cummins (1995).

2. **How do we measure quality of life?** In their review of the literature, Hughes et al. (1995) found that of the 87 studies evaluated, an interview, questionnaire, or a combination of the two were used in 74 percent of the studies. I have suggested a two-factor measurement model (see Table 12.4) based on the core quality of life dimensions and three measurement techniques (participant observation, performance-based assessment, and standardized instruments). Other investigators have suggested different measurement models. For example, Heal and Sigelman in this volume (see Table 10.1) suggest a measurement taxonomy that includes three components: general method, respondent, and type of instrument. Heal et al. (1995) have also suggested a 3 perceiver (individual, intimate acquaintance, or third party) by 3 perspectives (individual, intimate social relationships, or society at large) matrix. The common message in these measurement models is clear: the need to use multiple methods and assess quality of life from a number of different perspectives. Consensus on this issue will undoubtedly be pursued vigorously during the next few years.

3. **What psychometric standards need to be considered?** Regardless of our answers to the first two measurement issues, one cannot overlook the need to measure the quality of life construct reliably and validly. Although discussed briefly earlier in this chapter, a number of key points about necessary psychometric standards need to be reiter-

ated. First, the construct must be measured reliably, which requires investigators to demonstrate the consistency of their measures—whether the determination is made for test-retest, inter/intraobserver, or internal consistency. Second, the construct must be measured validly. Content validity is probably not enough. Investigators need to go one step further and demonstrate construct validity, which answers the question, "Do the items measure the underlying construct being studied?" This is the measurement issue that makes reaching consensus on the four conceptual issues discussed earlier in this section so important: Unless the quality of life construct and its indicators are conceptualized clearly, then measuring that construct is very difficult. And the third key point is that, if comparisons are made, then the investigator is obligated to develop and present standardization data.

4. **How do we overcome measurement challenges?** People with mental retardation and closely related disabilities present significant measurement challenges including the use of proxies, the basis for the list of specific life circumstances to be evaluated, the risk of acquiescence, the tendency toward socially desirable responding, the lack of effective communication systems, the potential contamination between the predictor and criterion variables, and demonstrated validity. One also needs to look at the effects of the interview itself. For example, Antaki and Rapley (1995) have recently used conversation analysis to show that the typical administration of quality of life questionnaires involves distortions of the questions brought about by the need to paraphrase complex items and distortions of answers brought about by interviewers' pursuit of legitimate answers. Similarly, Stancliffe (1995) recently reported moderate to low concordance rates between self-reports and reports by proxies.

I suggest the following strategies for overcoming some of these measurement problems:

- Use multiple methods to capture the core quality of life dimensions and their indicators that one is interested in.

- Use either-or questions or objective multiple choice questions with three or four options accompanied by pictures (Sigelman et al., 1993).

- Correct statistically for response biases (Harner & Heal, 1993; Heal, Borthwick-Duffy, & Saunders, 1995; Heal & Chadsey-Rusch, 1985).

- Use proxies (Heal & Sigelman, this volume; Schalock, 1994; Schalock & Keith, 1993).

- Resolve differences between the client and proxy through discussions and detailed behavioral observation (Stancliffe, 1995).

- Rely more heavily on participant observation that encompasses the issues of expressed choices, control, and satisfaction (Parsons & Reid, 1990; Realon, Favell, & Lowere, 1990).

- Ensure that there is little or no contamination between the predictor and criterion variables. Two criteria should guide our work here: the variables are not correlated; and the results are not an artifact of the method used. General guidelines to meet these two criteria include predictors that do not overlay conceptually; assessments that are separate so there is no articulation or communication between the instruments; and temporal independence between the predictors and the criterion (Schalock, 1995).

Conclusion: Quality of Life as an Organizing Concept

The major argument in this chapter is that we need to move away from viewing quality of life as an entity, and consider it instead a process and an organizing concept that can guide us in our work to improve the life conditions of all persons. It has also been argued that we need to move away from the historically-based notion of a distinction between subjective and objective indicators of quality of life, moving instead to the position that there are a number of core consensual quality of life dimensions, whose indicators can be measured by one of three measurement techniques: participant observation, performance-based assessment, or standardized instruments. If these arguments are valid, then there are at least three significant implications for the quality of life movement.

The first implication is that quality of life needs to be conceptualized as composed of a number of core dimensions that are based on empirical studies and experiential reports. The eight suggested in this chapter include: emotional well-being, interpersonal relations, material well-being, personal development, physical well-being, self-determination, social inclusion, and rights. It is important to stress that these core dimensions are important to all people, and should not be viewed differently for persons with disabilities. However, it is also essential to realize that these core dimensions are culturally based and may well differ across primary culture groups.

The second implication is that each of these core dimensions has a number of indicators that can serve as the basis for either assessing or evaluating what historically have been considered either subjective or objective indicators. The critical difference argued in this chapter is not between the types of indicators, but the measurement techniques that one uses to evaluate them. The participant observation technique discussed should logically be used for those dimensions and indicators considered as more subjective; and the performance-based assessment or standardized instruments are most relevant for those dimensions and indicators considered more objective.

The third implication is that if the concept of quality of life is changed from an entity to an organizing concept, positive by-products will emerge:

- the ability to evaluate those core dimensions typically assumed to be associated with a life of quality

- a sense of reference and guidance in deciding service delivery issues that should be based on quality principles such as self-determination, equity, opportunities, empowerment, inclusion, knowing the person, and person-centered planning

- the ability to use the resulting data *not* for evaluating quality of life as an entity, but rather for assessing the person's level of satisfaction or well-being, completing needs assessments, assessing outcomes, providing formative feedback to the various stakeholders, providing the overriding principle for program development or change, developing policy, or conducting research

- a continuing caution against imposing an objective standard that can be used to define a life of quality

In conclusion, the concept of quality is elusive, imprecise, and ever-changing. In this volume we have seen that the emerging consensus suggests that (a) there are a number of core quality of life principles; (b) there are a number of core quality of life dimensions; (c) each dimension (or its indicator) can be measured at either the subjective or objective level; and (d) valid quality of life measurement requires using a multi-dimensional approach. Despite these advances, a number of critical points remain to be discussed and researched. Quality of life is a complex concept due to its multiple perspectives, multiple dimensions, and multiple uses. Thus, there is continuous need for discussion, debates, research, and consumer input. Also, this is a critical time in both the history of approaches to persons with mental retardation and closely related disabilities and in how our society views people who are different by any criterion. Quality of life is a fundamental principle and process that is applicable to society as a whole and thus provides us with a valuable bridge for common understanding and good.

References

The Accreditation Council on Services for People with Disabilities (1993). *Outcome based performance measures.* Landover, MD: Author.

Andrews, F. R., & Whithey, S.B. (1976). *Social indicators of well-being. Americans' perceptions of life quality.* New York: Plenum Press.

Antaki, C., & Rapley, M. (1995). Questions and answers in psychological assessment schedules: Hidden troubles in 'quality of life' interviews. Personal correspondence.

Borthwick-Duffy, S. (1990). Quality of life of persons with severe and profound mental retardation. In R.L. Schalock (Ed.), *Quality of life: Perspectives and issues* (pp. 177-189). Washington, DC: American Association on Mental Retardation.

Brown, R.I., Bayer, M., & McFarlane, C. (1989). *Rehabilitation programmes: Performance and quality of life of adults with developmental handicaps.* Toronto: Lugus Productions.

Campbell, A. (1976). Subjective measures of well-being. *American Psychologist, 31,* 117-124.

Campbell, A., Converse, P.E., & Rogers, W.L. (1976). *The quality of American life.* New York: Sage.

Chen, S.T. (1988). Subjective quality of life in the planning and evaluation of programs. *Evaluation and Program Planning, 11,* 123-134.

Cummins, R.A. (1995). Assessing quality of life. In R.I. Brown (Ed.), *Quality of life for handicapped people* (pp. 102-120). London: Chapman & Hall.

Cummins, R.A., McCabe, M.P., Romeo, Y., & Gullone, E. (1994). The Comprehensive Quality of Life Scale: Instrument development and psychometric evaluation on tertiary staff and students. *Educational and Psychological Measurement, 54,* 372-382.

Edgerton, R.B. (1990). Quality of life from a longitudinal research perspective. In R.L. Schalock (Ed.), *Quality of life: Perspectives and issues* (pp.149-160). Washington, DC: American Association on Mental Retardation.

Evans, D.R., Burns, J.E., Robinson, W.E., & Garrett, O.J. (1985). The quality of life questionnaire: A multi-dimensional measure. *American Journal of Community Psychology, 13,* 305-322.

Flanagan, J.C. (1982). Measurement of quality of life: Current state of the art. *Archives of Physical Medicine and Rehabilitation, 63,* 56-59.

Goode, D.A. (1990). Measuring the quality of life of persons with disabilities: Some issues and suggestions. *News and Notes, 3,* 2, 6. American Association on Mental Retardation.

Goode, D.A. (Ed.) (1994). *Quality of life for persons with disabilities: International perspectives and issues.* Boston: Brookline Books.

Halpern, A.S., Nave, G., Close, D.W., & Nelson, D.J. (1986). An empirical analysis of the dimensions of community adjustment for adults with mental retardation. *Australia and New Zealand Journal of Developmental Disabilities, 12,* 147-157.

Harner, C.J., & Heal, L.W. (1993). The Multifaceted Lifestyle Satisfaction Scale (MLSS): Psychometric properties of an interview schedule for assessing personal satisfaction of adults with limited intelligence. *Research in Developmental Disabilities, 14,* 221-236.

Heal, L.W., Borthwick-Duffy, S.A., & Saunders, R.R. (1995). Assessment of quality of life. In J.W. Jacobson & J.A. Mulick (Eds.). *Manual of diagnosis and professional practice in mental retardation.* Washington, DC: American Psychological Association.

Heal, L.W., & Chadsey-Rusch, J. (1985). The lifestyle satisfaction scale (LSS): Assessing individuals' satisfaction with residence, community setting, and associated services. *Applied Research in Mental Retardation, 6,* 475-490.

Heal, L.W., Rubin, S.S., & Park, W. (1995). *Lifestyle Satisfaction Scale.* Champaign-Urbana, IL: Transition Research Institute, University of Illinois.

Himmel, P.B. (1984). Functional assessment strategies in clinical medicine: The care of arthritic patients. In C.V. Granger & C.E. Gresham (Eds.), *Functional assessment in rehabilitative medicine* (pp. 343-363). Baltimore: Williams & Wilkins.

Hughes, C., Hwang, R., Kim, J-H, Eisenman, L.T., & Killian, D.J. (1995). Quality of life in applied research: A review and analysis of empirical measures. *American Journal on Mental Retardation, 99,* 623-641.

Jamieson, J. (1993). *Adults with mental handicap: Their quality of life.* Vancover: British Columbia Ministry of Social Services.

Keith, K.D., Heal, L.W., & Schalock, R.L. (in press). Cross-cultural measurement of critical quality of life concepts. *Australia and New Zealand Journal of Developmental Disabilities.*

Keith, K.D., Yamamoto, M., Okita, N., & Schalock, R.L. (1995). Cross-cultural quality of life: Japanese and American college students. *Social Behavior and Personality, 23,* 163-170.

Keith, K.D., & Schalock, R.L. (1995). *Quality of student life questionnaire.* Worthington, OH: IDS Publishing Co.

Murrell, S.A., & Norris, F.H. (1983). Quality of life as the criterion for need assessment and community psychology. *Journal of Community Psychology, 11,* 88-97.

Parsons, M.B., & Reid, D.H. (1990). Assessing food preferences among persons with profound mental retardation: Providing opportunities to make choices. *Journal of Applied Behavior Analysis, 23,* 183-195.

Realon, R.E., Favell, J.E., & Lowere, A. (1990). The effects of making choices on engagement levels with persons who are profoundly multiple handicapped. *Education and Training in Mental Retardation, 25,* 299-305.

Saunders, R.R., & Spradlin J.E. (1991). A supported routine approach to active treatment for enhancing independence, competence, and self-worth. *Behavior Residential Treatment, 6,* 11-37.

Schalock, R.L. (1990). Attempts to conceptualize and measure quality of life. In R.L. Schalock (Ed.), *Quality of life: Perspectives and issues* (pp. 141-148). Washington, DC: American Association on Mental Retardation.

Schalock, R.L. (1994). Quality of life, quality enhancement, and quality assurance: Implications for program planning and evaluation in the field of mental retardation and developmental disabilities. *Evaluation and Program Planning, 17,* 121-131.

Schalock, R.L. (1995). *Outcome-based evaluation.* New York: Plenum Publishing Corporation.

Schalock, R.L., Bartnik, E., Wu, F., Konig, A., Lee, C.S., & Ritter, S. (1990). *An international perspective on quality of life measurement and use.* Paper presented at the meeting of the Association on Mental Retardation, Atlanta, GA.

Schalock, R.L., & Jansen, C.M. (1986). Assessing the goodness-of-fit between persons and their environments. *Journal of the Association for Persons with Severe Handicaps, 11,* 103-109.

Schalock, R.L., & Keith, K.D. (1993). *Quality of life questionnaire.* Worthington, OH: IDS Publishing Co.

Schalock, R.L., Keith, K.D., Hoffman, K., & Karan, O.C. (1989). Quality of life: Its measurement and use. *Mental Retardation, 27,* 25-31.

Sigelman, C.K., Schoenrock, C.J., Budd, E.C., Winer, J.L., Spanhel, C.L., Martin, P.O., Hromas, S., & Bensberg, G.J. (1983). *Communicating with mentally retarded persons: Asking questions and getting answers.* Lubbock: Texas Tech University, Research and Training Center in Mental Retardation.

Spitzer, W.O. (1987). State of Science in 1986: Quality of life and functional status as target variables for research. *Journal on Chronic Disease, 40,* 465-471.

Stancliffe, R.J. (1995). Assessing opportunities for choice-making: A comparison of self- and staff reports. *American Journal of Mental Retardation, 99,* 418-429.

Thorndike, E.L. (1939). *Your city.* New York: Harcourt, Brace.

Zautra, A.J., & Goodhart, D. (1979). Quality of life indicators: A review of the literature. *Community Mental Health Review, 19,* 4-10.